The aim of t[...]
is to make ava[...]
of classic titles by wel[...]
particular emphasis on making these books [...]
to Eastern Europe and the Two-Thirds World.

Trinitarian Doctrine
for Today's Mission

Trinitarian Doctrine
for Today's Mission

LESSLIE
NEWBIGIN

paternoster
press

First published in the UK 1963 by Edinburgh House Press

This edition published 1998 by
Paternoster Press in the Biblical Classics Library

04 03 02 01 00 99 98   7 6 5 4 3 2 1

Paternoster Press is an imprint of Paternoster Publishing,
P.O. Box 300, Carlisle, Cumbria, CA3 0QS, UK.

British Library Cataloguing in Publication Data

A catalogue record for this book is available from
the British Library

ISBN 0–85364–797–6

Printed in Great Britain by Mackays of Chatham PLC, Kent

CONTENTS

INTRODUCTION

In his autobiography[1] Lesslie Newbigin ruefully remarks about this book that, 'My hope was that it would provide the basis for a post-integration sequel to *One Body*[2]—a manifesto, in fact, for the new Division of World Mission and Evangelism. But it was not to be. Wim (General Secretary of the World Council of Churches) disapproved of its theology and my colleagues in the Division were not sufficiently persuaded to support me.'

This would be most unfortunate, because the significance of the book can now be seen to lie not simply in the fact that it provides a stepping-stone between an earlier post-Tambaram[3] concentration on a church-centred understanding of mission and an understanding of mission within the framework of a fully trinitarian appreciation of the work of God in the world. The latter idea would be fully explored by Newbigin almost twenty years later in *The Open Secret*, but even in 1963 one can see many important themes of his 1980s work: the concept of the re-evangelization of the West (though that phrase is not used), the imperative of applying Christian ethical insights to public life, resisting the 'privatization' of the Gospel, and so on.

Nor does the book's interest lie in the way in which Newbigin, having issued a pro-integration rallying call in *One Body, One Church, One World* (1958) is now trying to execute a delicate

---

1. *Unfinished Agenda* (Geneva: WCC, 1985) pp. 198–9.
2. *One Body, One Church, One World* (Edinburgh House Press, 1958).
3. The International Missionary Council meeting held in Tambaram, Madras 1938. See conference volumes (Edinburgh House Press, 1939).

piece of ecumenical footwork to ensure that the former IMC constituency is fully integrated into the work of the WCC, and that the WCC takes on its missionary responsibility by pointing to the burning issues for ordinary lay men and women and the reasons for their crisis of faith. In fact, in wrestling with the implications for Christian missions of the fracturing of Christendom, the end of the Social Gospel and belief in the inevitable progress of humankind towards a better future and the rise of revolutionary movements, Newbigin underestimates the hunger which *Honest to God*[4] would expose. Nor is it in the way that, on the one hand, in his passionate appeal to focus on the Father's providence and purpose and move away from exclusively Christocentric theology, he anticipates the famous ' paradigm shift' of John Hick, whilst on the other, by emphasizing the work of the Spirit, he encourages the emerging Pentecostal churches to feel at home in Geneva.

Though these aspects of the book are important, its real significance, and the reason why it merits re-printing, is the way in which Christian responsibility and the mission and unity of the church are grounded in the timeless trinitarian truths of the Christian faith. Particular attention should be paid to the appeal for sounder biblical models for mission and for greater development of trust in the work of the Spirit.

Eleanor Jackson

---

4. J.H. Robinson, *Honest to God* (SCM, 1963) engulfed the Western churches in a wave of questioning so that Newbigin's questions about the activity of God in the work got swallowed up in the debate about whether God existed at all.

PREFACE

This small essay is offered—as the title of the series indicates—as an invitation to discussion rather than as the announcement of conclusions. It arises from reflection on constant discussion of missionary problems and deals, I hope, with real issues. But, as the reader will quickly see, it lacks the depth and solidity which can come only where there is time for much wider reading around the issues discussed. It owes an immense amount to discussion with my colleagues on the staff of the World Council and to comments kindly sent in writing by many friends. Without a great deal of help and encouragement from Dr. Paul Löffler it would not have appeared at all, and to him I owe especial thanks. But I must emphasize the fact that it is a purely personal essay written in the hope that others more competent than I may decide whether it is useful.

It is addressed to those who are concerned with and committed to the missionary task. It is in no sense an apologia for missions; it is not addressed to those who ask 'Why missions?', even though some of their questions come up for hearing. It is an attempt to wrestle with perplexities which arise out of the present situation of missions for those most deeply committed to them.

It is not written to advocate any particular line of action, but rather as an effort to understand. No apology is needed for this. We must see before we can act rightly. If the vision is right, we shall know how to act. If this essay in understanding is at fault, the writer hopes to be corrected.

I: Missions in an Ecumenical Perspective

We shall begin with the event which took place at New Delhi in November 1961, when the International Missionary Council and the World Council of Churches became one body. That event was the outward sign and fruit of a process of thinking which had been developing during the previous twenty-five years. If one looks for a point from which to mark the beginning of the process (and such points are always somewhat arbitrary), one would find it in the World Missionary Conference at Tambaram in 1938, with its emphatic announcement of a 'church-centric' view of the missionary task. The decades that followed the Tambaram Conference have witnessed a growing ecumenical consensus on the subject of the mission and unity of the Church. With a variety of accent and emphasis, ecumenical conferences have reiterated the conviction that the mission of the Church and its unity both belong to its proper character, because the Church is that body in which God wills to reconcile all mankind to himself.

Several strands of experience have contributed to these expressions of the nature of the missionary task. The experience of the missionary movement during the past two hundred years, and as its fruit, the coming into existence of Churches in all parts of the world, have brought about a slow shift of perspective in the thinking about the Church even among those not directly involved in missions. The rise of the ecumenical movement, itself in large part a product of this missionary experience, has created a new context for the missionary task. Events in the

Western world, especially in Europe, have destroyed from men's minds the concept of society as a *corpus Christianum*. The tendency towards practical identification of the influence of the European nations with the influence of Christianity which appears in some missionary writing before 1914 is no longer possible. The Western world has had to be recognized once again as a mission field, and the Churches have been compelled in a new way to define their nature and mission as parts of a divine society distinct from the wider society of nations in which they live, and all these factors have contributed to developments in the field of theology in the direction of a missionary understanding of the nature of the Church itself. The truth that the Church is itself something sent into the world, the continuation of Christ's mission from the Father, something which is not so much an institution as an expedition sent to the ends of the earth in Christ's name, has been grasped with a new vividness. Among those who have reflected about these matters it becomes less and less possible to speak of the missionary task otherwise than as the embassage of the whole people of God to the whole world.

At the same time there are factors, distinct though not unrelated, which reinforce this movement of thought. The shift in the balance of political power in the world, the attack on 'colonialism' and the rise to independent nationhood of the peoples among whom foreign missionary work was conducted, all combine to discourage patterns of missionary thinking which assume a Western base. Missions can hardly claim to be respectable at the present time unless they take pains to disown publicly the patterns of colonialism. Such influences as these from the secular world powerfully reinforce the movements within the life and thought of the Church towards an understanding of missions in terms of the mission of the whole Church to the whole world.

This understanding is assumed as the starting point of the present discussion. Let it be said plainly that this does not mean that such an understanding of the task is generally operative in the practical work of missions. It is not. And it must be added that the dichotomy between public statement and day-to-day practice in this matter is likely to become (to quote a paper accepted by the Commission at New Delhi) 'morally debilitating' to the whole missionary movement if it is not tackled urgently. Under the title 'Joint Action for Mission' the Commission is committed during the coming years to a sustained effort to assist Churches and missions to move from talk to action in this matter. But the fact of integration, by which the World Council of Churches becomes responsible for the kind of missionary discussion hitherto promoted by the International Missionary Council, does effectively symbolize the acceptance of this conception of the missionary task and ensures that discussion begins from it. This is where we shall begin.

II: The Limits of Ecumenicity—the Question of Truth

The integration of the International Missionary Council and the World Council is an event in the field of relationships. It provides, as those who have advocated it believe, a set of relationships which will be helpful in the reshaping of missionary action—in the direction of a pattern more exactly conformed than the present pattern to the understanding of the nature of the missionary task which we share. But behind these questions of pattern there are deeper questions of substance, and these are questions which must now be faced. Why is there not more vigour in the missionary work of the Churches which share in the ecumenical movement? Why does the call to foreign missionary service not evoke a response from more of the ablest students in the universities? Let it be granted that part of the answer lies in the field of relationships, in the fact that the patterns of missionary action do not conform to the facts of the Gospel or of the world today; the question has still to be asked: 'Is there not a deeper reason? Is there not a deep uncertainty in the Churches concerning the uniqueness and finality of the Gospel itself?

That there should be hesitancy among minds sensitive to the spiritual atmosphere of our time is not surprising, for one of the most obvious facts of our time is the dominance of a spirit of relativism in matters of religion. Not since the Christianization of Europe after the time of Constantine has Western man had the experience of living in a world of religious pluralism such as the present. Certainly the great religions of Asia have existed for

14

millennia, but Western man was for long almost wholly isolated from contact with them. And even when contact began to be made, the cultural situation was such that those religions had very little opportunity to make an impact on the mind of Western men comparable to the impact of Christianity upon them. It is true that among an *élite* of scholars from the eighteenth century onwards the discovery of—especially—Chinese philosophy made a tremendous impact, which in turn affected the general direction of Western thinking. But it is only in our day that the means of travel and communication have been such as to break down for ordinary men the barriers that separate the world religions. For the Western supporters of missions in the nineteenth century the men of other religions were remote figures, objects of compassion or of curiosity, but not the bearers of an alternative view of life which could seriously challenge the spiritual security of Western man.

Now, however, the situation is wholly different. The religions are no longer insulated from each other by distance. Students from every part of the world and from every religious community jostle one another on the campuses of Western universities, share the same studies, the same books, the same discussions of world affairs. The great international and inter-governmental organizations, both the United Nations itself and also its many specialist agencies, provide a sphere in which some of the ablest men of all religions are constantly co-operating in seeking the solution of the pressing problems of mankind. In UNESCO there is an organization which deliberately seeks to create the means for a common spiritual basis for the life of mankind. In a multitude of international conferences, for all sorts of commercial, scientific, and cultural purposes, men and women from all over the world meet as equals in a milieu in which any suggestion that absolute truth belongs to one of the many strands of human religious life seems simply absurd. And finally, for those who do not share in any of these opportunities for inter-cultural meeting, there is the ceaselessly growing flood of tourists which spreads over every accessible bit of the earth's surface, bringing ordinary men and women of every land into direct contact with each other, not to mention the movements of migrants, refugees and people forced by pressure of population to seek work in other lands.

It is not surprising if, in the face of these new experiences, some of the traditional supports for the missionary enterprise began to shake. For it must be frankly admitted that—whatever might be said from the pulpit about the true basis of missions in the Gospel itself—the motives with which they have been supported have been mixed. The very word 'mission' has come to suggest an operation in which one reaches down in pity and sympathy to the less fortunate, the unenlightened, the under-privileged. The picture of 'the heathen' to which Christians have responded with the devotion of their prayer and substance in the work of missions has too often been the picture of the poor, the ignorant, the diseased. To the extent that this has been so, it is not surprising that now, when one has a chance to meet 'the heathen' in the persons of the highly competent and cultured participants in the life of modern international society, there is a shaking of the traditional foundations.

Moreover, there is a very critical question addressed to the Church from those who are most sensitive to the spiritual situation of mankind. There are those who ask us whether, by continuing to insist upon the uniqueness and finality of the revelation of God in Christ, the Christian Church is not inca-pacitating itself to play its proper part in healing the divisions of mankind. To these critics it appears that missionary thinking— even when, it is in ecumenical terms—has simply failed to take account of the new situation of the human race. Humanity, it is argued, is now in a situation where it must learn to live as one community or perish. In all former ages of human history, mankind was divided into great cultural groups, effectively separated from one another by distance. In each of these groups religion was one of the great integrating factors making for cohesion, and stability. But the human race is now in a wholly different situation. There is no more separation. All parts of the human race are increasingly involved with one another in all phases of human activity. In this new situation the greatest need for mankind is to find a centre of cohesion capable of providing unity and stability for the human family as a whole. To take the religion of *one* of the great human groups—even if this religion now has some kind of foothold in all parts of the world—and claim for it that it is the proper faith for all mankind, is simply to prove oneself blind to the realities of the human situation. It is to invite a religious civil war just at the moment when mankind needs above all to find civil peace.

The question which thus arises does not merely come from outside the Christian Churches. It finds also an echo from within. It would be surprising if it did not, for Christians also live in this world. Moreover, there are reasons why the echo should be especially strong in those who have learned in the ecumenical movement how great is the enrichment which comes when, instead of attacking and excommunicating each other, we listen to each other. We have discovered many times in these years of inter-church discussion that even those who seemed to be contradicting us had something to teach us about Christ. We have seen walls of fear and suspicion crumble, and new ranges of experience open up in the wider fellowship into which we were brought. It is therefore understandable if the question is raised: 'Should not this process be extended further? May we not find that if we extend this kind of discussion we shall have yet more to learn, yet more enrichment of our fellowship? Is not the logical development of this whole movement something like a world fellowship of religions? Are we so sure as our predecessors were that there is salvation for mankind only by the explicit acceptance of the Name of Jesus Christ?

Plainly we come here to the central question, a question of ultimate truth. The ecumenical movement has grown out of the missionary movement. It has reached a point at which we have come to see the missionary task as the continuing work of him who was lifted up to draw all men to himself. Therefore we have come to see missions and unity as indissolubly connected. And now, having reached this point, we are compelled to recognize that we are confronted in a new way with one single question: the question of the uniqueness, sufficiency and finality of Jesus

Christ as the one Lord and Saviour of the world. This question is raised in two ways by our experience in the ecumenical movement. That is to say:

(*a*) When the missionary task is placed in a fully ecumenical setting, every other question except the question about Christ is in principle excluded. Every motive for missions to which one appeals must be one which is valid (in principle) equally for the Asian and for the European, equally for the Russian and for the American. Any open or covert suggestion, for instance, that missions are valuable as an insurance against Communism, or as an agency of technical aid to backward areas, is ruled out. By placing missions in a world-wide setting one commits oneself to the belief that the one essential question for all mankind is the question concerning Jesus Christ and that every other question which missions may raise is secondary.

(*b*) When the movement for unity is understood in missionary terms, then every other potential centre for human unity except Jesus Christ is ruled out. This means that we have to face the negative as well as the positive implication of the confession of Jesus as Lord. If it is Jesus only, Jesus in his concrete human reality who has been exalted to the right hand of God as king and head of the human race, then what was true of his earthly ministry will be true also of his continuing action through his Church—it both unites and separates. The words, 'I came not to bring peace but a sword,' will have to be accepted. If he is the one appointed by God to be the king of men, then all other claims to provide a final basis for human unity will have to be denounced as disobedience. If he is the concrete revelation of God's truth, then all that does not conform to that revelation will have to be exposed as false. Every proposal for unity among the religions rests upon some belief which may be open but is usually covert about what is ultimate truth. A proposal for a unity which includes both Christianity and other religions rests (openly or covertly) upon belief in some reality other than God's revelation in Jesus Christ. The experience of learning to listen to one another which the ecumenical movement has given us is certainly valid beyond the confines of Christendom. We have indeed to learn to enter into real conversation with men of other religions if they are to apprehend Jesus Christ as Saviour and if we are to learn all the manifold wisdom of God which he set forth in Jesus. But the ecumenical movement remains missionary through and through because it is a movement not for any kind of unity, but for that unity which is God's creation through the lifting up of Jesus Christ upon the Cross and through the continuing work of his Spirit.

One can put the same double point by making the following affirmations:

(*a*) The ecumenical movement remains open to *all* who confess Jesus Christ as God and Saviour. The movement springs from the faith that it is in Jesus Christ that God has chosen to unite all men to himself, and that therefore all who confess him ought to acknowledge one another as his, however great be the difference between them.

(*b*) The ecumenical movement remains open *only* to those who confess Jesus, Christ as God and Saviour. Because Jesus Christ is God's mercy-seat given for mankind, no other proposed basis for the unity of the human race can be accepted.

The openness of the ecumenical movement to all who confess Jesus as God and Saviour occasions criticism from those who believe that thereby questions of truth are being compromised; the restriction of the ecumenical movement to those who confess Jesus occasions criticism by those who believe that thereby human unity is hindered. The truth is that it is the very essence of this movement that the limits of its comprehensiveness are set, not by men but by God, because he has provided in Jesus Christ the one who is the only king and head of the human race. We may therefore neither disown those who acknowledge him nor acknowledge those who disown him.

To sum up what has been said so far, the development of the missionary movement, of the movement towards unity which has sprung from it, and the present consensus concerning the mission-in-unity of the Church, leave us face to face with one central question: Is Jesus Christ alone the Lord and Saviour of mankind, the king and head of the race? In a sense this is, of course, no new question, but the ancient question which the Gospel has always raised. The way in which it is raised today, however, is new in the experience of ordinary men and women in the Churches of the Western world. The ordinary church member is now in a position where he must be able, amid this pluralistic society in which the claims of all the religions to final truth compete openly in the life of society, to believe and affirm the final authority of Jesus Christ. Within the conditions of 'Christendom' this issue did not arise in quite the same way or with quite the same sharpness. For the vast majority within the Christian nations, the name of Jesus stood simply for the ultimate religious truth. That truth might be honoured or dishonoured, obeyed or disobeyed, but there was no serious religious rival. Today the affirmation of the final authority of Jesus must be made amid the clash of rival claims to religious truth and in a society which has become saturated with the idea that all truths are relative and partial.

There was a time when it was possible to support the work of missions without having seriously faced this question of religious truth. That time is past. There can be no recovery of vigour and directness in the work of missions so long as that question is not faced.

This study is written in the faith that Jesus is indeed the Lord and Saviour of all mankind. It is written out of the desire to confess him as Lord and thereby to give praise to God the Father, because he has not left us in the dark and in the bondage of sin, but has given us in his Son the revelation of himself and has delivered us, through him, from the power of evil. It is written in the faith that God the Holy Spirit can use even such human words to kindle faith and to illuminate what is dark and perplexing. It does not attempt to expand the implications of this faith otherwise than as they bear directly on our present, missionary obedience. Nor does it attempt an apologia for the Gospel in the face of the claims of its rivals. It is an attempt to face with as much honesty as possible the reasons for hesitancy in the thrust of the missionary movement and to draw the necessary conclusions for our understanding of the missionary task.

III: Occasions for Questioning Today: Where are Missions Going?

The causes which account for the spread of any faith are no doubt complex and mysterious. There is something more in them than anything that a calculus of sociological probabilities could account for. But one of the factors must surely be that their faith enables men to make some sort of sense of their experience. This is not the only factor; one could mention several others. But for the sustained vitality and converting power of any faith over a long period, this is surely indispensable.

Certainly the faith which appeals to the Bible is committed in principle to give some kind of interpretation, not only of inward and individual spiritual experience but also of the social and corporate life of man in history and of the natural world. Nothing less than this is implied in the doctrine that God created all things in Christ and will sum up all things in him. The Christian world mission cannot command whole-hearted and continuing commitment unless through participation in it men and women are persuaded that they are participating significantly in what God is doing for mankind as a whole. This is not to ask for an easy pragmatism, a faith simply in what 'works'. The sign by which the Christian makes sense of the world is the sign of the Cross. But we cannot commit ourselves, or ask others to commit themselves, wholly and finally to the missionary task unless we are able to see in some way how that task fits into the whole of what God is doing in the secular history of the world. A mission which is merely 'our effort', an affair about which we

21

can be optimistic or pessimistic, anxious or hopeful, an affair which is merely one of the various 'good causes' which one might support, is not the mission of God as the Bible portrays it. One cannot, for example, become a real missionary to the world of modern industry unless one is able in some measure to meet industrial man at the point where he is concerned, and show that the Christian faith can illuminate his world and give him power to act constructively in it. A missionary in industry must have some understanding, however tentative and groping, of what industry means in the purpose of God, what he is doing in it and how he would have us become his fellow workers in it. Similarly, to take another equally pertinent example, one cannot become a real missionary to a modern Hindu, involved in the struggles of his own nation, without meeting him at the point of his concern. One must be willing to wrestle with the things with which he is wrestling, and show how the Christian faith enables him to understand what God is doing to India and to Hinduism, and to find the resources to meet the demands of this time. Without this approach the missionary will seem to be a mere proselytizer, one who is seeking adherents for his cause and his opinions; he will seem to be one who comes simply to draw men out of their world into his, rather than one who comes into their world with the light that can illuminate it and the spiritual strength that can enable men to walk rightly in it.

What is true of these particular human situations is true of the missionary task seen as a whole. There cannot be sustained conviction in the prosecution of the missionary task if there is not some illumination—by faith, not by sight—of the way in which this task is related to God's whole purpose for the world. It is perhaps at this point that we may find the occasion for the present hesitancy in the missionary movement. For we have recently passed from a time when it seemed rather easy to interpret the place of the Christian world mission in the secular history of mankind to a time when it seems more difficult. For Western Christians during the century before 1914 it did seem that the movement of world history was in the same direction as the movement of the Christian mission—namely towards a more just, human and peaceful world order. They could believe that in pressing forward with the Christian missionary task they were moving with the forces of world history, forward towards a better future. But today this is no longer so. The idea of general universal progress has broken down, leaving behind either some sort of Utopian fanaticism—Marxist or other—or else scepticism and despair. For those who have not given way to despair and who have not accepted the Marxist interpretation of history, there does not seem to be any generally accepted alternative framework for the understanding of events. There is a vague feeling that things ought to get gradually better and that Christian missions ought to contribute to this betterment. If they do not do so, there is a feeling that one should look elsewhere. It may be all very well to have an inward experience of the love of God, but if it is not matched by any faith that the same loving purpose is operative in the world, the experience does not provide an enduring basis for missionary witness. When missions meet such shattering set-backs as have occurred in China, and when events seem to move towards similar experiences in other parts of the world, a doctrine of missions which has no doctrine of secular history breaks down.

It is illuminating in this connection to note the different ways in which the great world missionary conferences have approached their task. At Edinburgh in 1910 the sense of the world as a whole, of its ripeness for evangelization and of the imminence of the coming of the Kingdom of God, was uppermost. Both at the beginning and at the end the mysterious word of our Lord was quoted: 'There be some standing here . . . who shall not taste of death till they see the Kingdom of God come with power.' In the closing moments of the conference, Mott quoted the words,

> 'The work which centuries might have done
> Must crowd the hour of setting sun.'

Nothing less than the evangelization of the world *now* and the coming of the Kingdom of God was the key-note of Edinburgh's climactic utterances.

At the Jerusalem conference in 1928 the concern was still with the Kingdom of God, but it was thought of in a different way. 'The end is nothing less than the production of Christ-like character in individuals and societies and nations, through faith in and fellowship with Christ, the living Saviour, and through corporate sharing of life in a divine society.' The meeting was profoundly concerned with what was going on in the world and with the attempt to understand it from a Christian point of view. It devoted much attention to the rise of secularism and to its meaning for Christians. It reflected much of the same thinking which was later to lead to the Oxford Conference on Church, Community and State. Its closing words were of 'hope and expectation of His glorious Kingdom', though perhaps the whole context leads one to infer that for many of the delegates this kingdom was conceived rather in terms of 'a Christ-like world' than in terms of 'a new heaven and a new earth'.

By contrast the Tambaram meeting in 1938 was much more concerned with the Church. Its theme was 'The World Mission of the Church'. 'Notice,' said Dr. Mott in his opening address, 'it is the Church which is to be at the centre of our thinking and resolving these creative days—the Divine Society founded by Christ and His apostles to accomplish His will in the world.' And so it was to prove. The Tambaram meeting marked the beginning of an exceedingly necessary and fruitful period during which missionary thinking was, to use the oft repeated phrase, 'church-centric'. It is to the practical developments which arose out of the Tambaram meeting that we are largely indebted for that 'consensus' about mission and unity with which this essay began and which the Willingen meeting of 1952 also helped to develop.

But at Willingen there was also strong criticism of the exclusive 'church-centric' understanding of missions. The meeting wrestled with the question of the relation between God's work in the mission of his Church and his work in secular history, but was not able to come to a common mind. 'It is precisely at this point, where men ask the question: What is happening to us in our time? that they find it most impossible to take any account of

God's rule—whether they ask it with perplexity and despair or whether they ask it with compelling secular hope.'[1] During the succeeding decade Christians have wrestled with this question; how shall we understand what God is doing in the events of our time? And they have sensed that this is a central question for the understanding of the missionary task.

It is significant that at the New Delhi Assembly this was the issue on which it was hardest to find agreement. There were, on the one side, those who insisted that, because Christ is the Lord of history, he is at work in the events of our time; that we must expect to discern his working there; and it is there—in the world, among men in their ordinary lives—that we must find him: that he comes to meet us in the man of another faith and of no faith, with whom—therefore—we must engage not in monologue but in true dialogue. There were, on the other side, those who feared that language of this kind could lead to a sort of syncretism in which the distinctive claims of the Gospel would be compromised. The Assembly did not have the time to carry the discussion far, or even to achieve a real meeting of minds on the question. It is an urgent and necessary task to carry forward this discussion, for it is quite certain that there cannot be a convincing affirmation of the authority of Christ which does not illuminate the relation between Christ's sovereignty and the events of secular history.

We must grant that the period of missionary history dominated by the 'church-centric' understanding of missions had been fruitful. It has brought us to our present consensus regarding the unity and mission of the Church and it has been the presupposition of the events that have led to the integration of the World Council of Churches and the International Missionary Council. But a church-centric doctrine and practice of mission can also be the occasion of misunderstanding. The Church is indeed the agent of God's mission and a clue to his dealing with mankind, but this does not mean that the work of God in the world is to be simply identified with the progress of

1. See Norman Goodall (ed.), *Missions under the Cross* (Edinburgh House Press, 1953), p. 239.

the Church in mission, and unity. It does not mean that the
events of secular history are mere background for the story of
the Church, or merely scenery for the drama of salvation.

Plainly the Bible does not permit us to look at the matter in
this way. The Gospel of God, with which both Testaments are
concerned, does not refer merely to one of the strands of man's
cultural history. It refers to the beginning and end of all things
and therefore to the real meaning of all that happens. It follows
that there cannot be an absolute separation between the history
of our redemption, and the sacred story of the Old and New
Testaments, the story of the Church and the whole story of
mankind. The Bible does not make such a separation. The point
here is not merely the obvious one that the story of Israel is
intertwined with that of the pagan nations round about. It is that
the whole history of these pagan nations is in the hands of God
and is propelled by him towards the end which he has revealed
to his own people. When Israel is told 'You are my witnesses'
(e.g. Is. 44:8), it is plain that Israel is not being summoned to
help God to cope with the otherwise unmanageable powers of
the pagan empires, or to organize a movement which will carry
out God's purposes in contradistinction to the godless purposes
of these empires. They are but a little thing in God's hands. He
raises them up and casts them down as he will. Israel's rôle is to
be—precisely—witness of his purpose to these pagan nations to
whom it would be otherwise unintelligible. Israel knows what
God is doing—or ought to know; the others do not. The
revelation of his nature and will which God has given to Israel
equips her to understand the meaning of what he is doing.

The New Testament carries on the same teaching. Christians
are not called upon to organize a movement to counter the
powers of paganism. They are called upon to be witnesses to him
who is sovereign over history, whose character and will have been
revealed and who—in Christ—has done the deed which precipitates the final issue for all mankind. They are called upon to
recognize the signs of the times—that is to say the signs of the
last days which follow the coming of Jesus and point to his
coming again. In the light of what Jesus has done they will

understand that war, tumult, persecution and suffering, the appearing of false messiahs and the manifesting of the antichrist with all his deceitful powers, are not evidence of defeat for the Christian cause, but are among the things which 'must come to pass'. There is a close parallelism between these words and the words which the Lord speaks about his own sufferings. To these also there is the term 'must' attached. They are a necessary part of the birth of a new order. And so are the sufferings of the world. The coming of the Messiah precipitates the crisis of human history. In him God presents every man, and the whole of mankind, with the possibility of receiving or rejecting the end for which he created all things. The whole of human history, after the coming of Christ until his coming again, is the pressing of this choice to the final issue. And the Church is the body which understands this, which is called to bear witness among the nations to the real meaning of the events amid which we live, and thereby to present to all men and nations the concrete alternatives of acceptance or rejection.

It must be confessed that in some of our thinking about the task of missions we have taken a wholly unbiblical view of the world. We have spoken as though the affairs of secular history concerned us only when they either assisted or impeded the work of the Church. We have often made it appear as though we believed God to be interested only in religious questions. Thereby we have repelled from the Gospel the artist and the scientist and the lover of men, because we appeared to be insensitive to the beauty, the truth and the goodness that they found everywhere about them; because it appeared that we tried to assert the uniqueness of Christ by denying the splendour of God's work in creation and in the spirit of men. We have made it appear that we have regarded the man who gives himself to the service of God and men in politics or social service or research as having a less central part in God's purpose than the man who gives full-time service to the Church. In the operations of missions we have made it appear that we regard a doctor in a mission hospital as doing 'God's work' in a sense in which a doctor in a government hospital was not.

But if we avoid the error of denying God's work in the world outside the Church, we have also to avoid the opposite error, which is so to identify the dynamic movements of secular history with the work of God that one judges the 'relevance' of the work of the Church by the measure in which it relates itself to these movements. It is not enough simply to affirm that God is at work in the affairs of the secular world—for instance in the revolutionary movements of our time. If we believe in the sovereign governance of all things by God, and if we believe that all that is good comes from him, we are bound to agree that, in some sense, he is at work in these movements, in the movements of national liberation, of scientific discovery, of cultural renaissance and —certainly—in the movements of rebirth and reform in the non-Christian religions. But it is not sufficient to leave the matter there. We must go on to ask 'In what sense?' If we do not, it will be a very short step from saying, 'God is at work in these movements' to saying, 'It is enough to be involved actively in these movements in order to be in line with the will of God.' The more attractive and impressive the movement is, the more easily will this happen.

That way lies sheer paganism. It means in the end that every kind of vitality is accepted as a manifestation of the divine. In the field of history it leads to the deification of success. Charles Cochrane[2] has shown how the classical attempt to formulate a philosophy of history came to an end with the concept of 'fortune'. When Rome, fortune's favourite, fell, nothing was left of the philosophy. There will presumably always be movements in human history the protagonists of which imagine that success is the only justification that they need. Such high-sounding phrases as 'the logic of history' may easily cover the same banal paganism as Rome's 'fortune'. But a Christian cannot possibly identify the purpose of God with whatever is currently the successful political line—imperial, anti-colonial or any other. The Church should by this time have learned that it is normal for it to work 'against the stream'.

---

2. *Christianity and Classical Culture* (Oxford University Press, 1944), p. 474.

But what is 'the stream'? Is that not also under God's government? Is it not also part of that 'all' which is to be summed up in Christ? Is it not part of that 'all' creation which was 'through Christ'? It is common to hear theologians speak of the Gospel as God's 'intervention' in human history. But is God absent from human history apart from this intervention? Is the world outside the Church, 'an atheistical patch in the universe'? Is God not at work in the affairs of the world outside the bounds of the body that confesses Christ as Saviour? The Bible does not allow us to doubt that he is. But how? In what terms shall we affirm the uniqueness, sufficiency and finality of Christ without either denying the reality of his working in the world or blunting the sharpness of the challenge which he puts to every man to choose?

It is at this point, I believe, that the real difficulties lie for those in the Asian Churches who are trying to reopen a living dialogue through which the Gospel can be commended to men of other faiths and of no faith. In the older Churches of the West it may well be that syncretism is the real danger; there seem to be many who think it only natural that the usual list of religious allegiances—Roman Catholic, Protestant and Jewish—should be extended as the occasion arises to include Hindus, Muslims and Buddhists also. But this kind of syncretism is not a living danger in the Churches of Asia. Here the danger, as their leaders have often pointed out, is 'ghettoism'—a practical withdrawal into the position of a tolerated and static minority, a cultural and religious enclave within the majority community. Correspondingly the great need is to find ways of breaking out of this isolation and of entering into real dialogue with the men of other faiths who are wrestling with the problems of the modern world and who are seeking resources to meet its demands.

In this situation, to reopen the famous debate concerning the continuity or discontinuity of the Gospel with the religions of mankind is not helpful to the Asian Churches. There is little temptation to go back to the kind of thinking which called for Kraemer's famous and decisive proclamation of the uniqueness and otherness of the Gospel. What is needed now, if there is to be a living dialogue with men of other faiths, is that we should see how God's unique and saving revelation of himself in Jesus Christ enables men to interpret what is happening to them and to respond to the calling of God in the midst of the life of the world. The mere assertion of discontinuity, true as it is, necessary as it is in certain contexts, is not the word which is required at this moment. What is required is an understanding of the relation between what God has done—uniquely and finally—in Christ and what he is doing in the life of mankind as a whole; an understanding which will enable Christians to communicate the Gospel in words and patterns of living which are in accordance with what God is doing, and is calling men to do, in their secular life.

Clearly it is impossible in a short paper to discuss this question as a whole. That is a task beyond the competence of any single human being. It calls for the concerted work of Christians in many different areas of life. No more is attempted here than to try to face some of the questions which arise specifically for those responsible for the work of missions; questions concerning the relation between what is happening in the world and what God is doing in the missionary work of the Church. By way of illustration I suggest three such questions; obviously there are others which might have been chosen.

(*a*) There was a time when it seemed possible to believe that, as the result of missionary endeavour, more and more peoples would be brought into the Church and that the life of the nations would be brought more and more under the power of the Gospel. An expectation of this kind seems to underlie much of what was said at the great missionary conference of 1910 with a hope that if only all the forces of Christendom could be properly mobilized for the task, very much greater progress in this direction could be made. It was a reasonable hope in the circumstances of the time. The experience of the 'Great Century' during which the vast expansion of Christianity in Asia and Africa took place could be adduced as solid ground for it. But events in the recent past have seemed to shake it. China, the area of the greatest single effort in modern missions, has been abruptly closed. The Indian historian of Asia's experience under Western dominance, K. M. Panikkar, concludes his survey with a chapter entitled 'The Failure of Christian Missions'. Large parts of formerly 'Christian' lands are now firmly controlled by Communist governments which seek by all means to destroy the Church. Even where Christian expansion continues, it does not keep pace with the growth of population. Proportionately to the human race as a whole, Christians are a diminishing minority. It does not *look* as if Christianity were the clue to the future of the human race.

(*b*) It is not only that Christians are a diminishing minority. It is also that the area of human life in which Christianity has authority seems to be shrinking. More and more realms of life appear to be taken over by systems of thought and organization which take no account whatever of religious questions. Even a zealous Christian working in a vast modern factory finds it hard to see where anything that he can say about Jesus has any relevance. The family problems which in a former day were unhesitatingly taken to the parish priest are now likely to go to the psychiatric social worker provided by the local authority. The African migrating from the village where the Church was the centre of the common life to a 'location' dominated by the shafts and slag heaps of the diamond or copper mines finds himself thrown into a turmoil of affairs for which nothing that the Church taught him seems to offer any guidance. The Chinese students suddenly swept up into the tide of Communist 'liberation' bitterly accuse their missionary teachers for having deceived them about the real character of power in the world. It is not just that Christians are—relatively—a shrinking minority, but also that—even for those who are Christians—it seems to be a shrinking part of human experience in respect of which Christianity has authority.

(*c*) Moreover those who know the work of missions best are most aware of the ambivalent character of their fruits. With a vast expenditure of lives and resources the Church has been planted in most parts of the world. But it remains in the greater number of places a small and apparently peripheral community.

The great masses of Asia remain apparently impervious to the appeal of the Gospel. The Churches are, to outward seeming, very much like Western cultural colonies precariously situated on the edge of the old societies, tolerated chiefly because they show no signs of threatening the old faiths. They are heavily dependent, both spiritually and financially, on continuing support from the West. They are divided along the lines of the historic cultural divisions of Western Europe and, in spite of some movements towards unity, they show very little sign of becoming strong united and uniting bodies within the cultural life of their nations. They show little power of spontaneous growth and depend rather upon a continual flow of resources from outside to keep them where they are. Though eyes of faith may see them as the first-fruits of the people of Asia and Africa, eyes not so lighted will be inclined to write them off as the ineffectual remnants of the era of Western dominance—comparable to the little communities of eastern Christians that survived the end of the first great missionary period of Christianity and the rise of the power of Islam.

I do not suggest that these questions are more than illustrations of the grounds for hesitancy among those who care for the missionary work of the Church. But they are real and important. How are they to be answered?

IV: The Relevance of Trinitarian Doctrine

The purpose of the chapters which follow is to show that there are resources for the meeting of these perplexities within the Christian understanding of God as Father, Son and Holy Spirit, to invite the missionary movement to bind to itself afresh the strong Name of the Trinity. We have stated that the present situation of the missionary movement has brought us to the point where the question of the uniqueness and finality of Christ is presented with a new sharpness. We have now to say that this question will not be rightly answered, nor will the question of the relation between what God is doing in the mission of the Church and what he is doing in the secular events of history be rightly answered, except within the framework of a fully and explicitly trinitarian doctrine of God.

This statement may not, at first sight, appear to contain anything which is not familiar to all Christians. But the familiar may sometimes be rendered inoperative just by its familiarity. The point has several times been made that a true doctrine of missions must make a large place for the work of the Holy Spirit; but it is equally true that a true doctrine of missions will have much to say of God the Father. The opinion may be ventured that recent ecumenical thinking about the mission and unity of the Church has been defective at both these points. The church-centric view of missions has perhaps been too exclusively founded upon the person and work of Christ and has perhaps done less than justice to the whole trinitarian doctrine of God. Such phrases as 'the Lordship of Christ over the Church and the

World', and such images as that of the building up of the body of Christ, have had almost exclusive occupancy of the central places in ecumenical thinking about the nature of the mission of the Church. We have already borne testimony to the immense importance and fruitfulness of this period of missionary thinking. But it may be that the time has come to ask whether it does not require some correction.

If one looks to the New Testament one certainly does not find a formally developed doctrine of the Trinity—any more than one finds other doctrines formally developed. But an attentive reader will note how constantly a trinitarian pattern underlies the language of St Paul, and how large a place is taken by the work of the Holy Spirit, and by the reference of all things finally to God the Father. And when the Church began to take the message of salvation through Jesus Christ out into the pagan world, it very soon found itself compelled to articulate a fully trinitarian doctrine of the God whom it proclaimed. It is indeed a significant fact that the great doctrinal struggles about the nature of the Trinity, especially about the mutual relations of the Son and the Father, developed right in the midst of the struggle between the Church and the pagan world. These trinitarian struggles were indeed an essential part of the battle to master the pagan world view at the height of its power and self-confidence. The Church had to articulate the Christian message of God's Kingdom in a world which interpreted human life mainly in terms of the interaction of 'virtue' and 'fortune'. Put in terms more relevant to our day, human life was interpreted as the interaction of man's intelligence, skill and courage with the forces of his environment. It is significant that the Church found itself driven to articulate the Christian message in this situation in terms of trinitarian doctrine, and that, during the period in which the intellectual struggle took place to state the Gospel in terms of Graeco-Roman culture without thereby compromising its central affirmation, it was the doctrine of the Trinity which was the key to the whole theological debate. In other words, it was in terms of this doctrine that Christians were able to state both the unity and the distinctness of God's work in the forces of man's environment and God's work of regeneration within the soul of man. The vehemence of the doctrinal struggles which centred on the formulation of the trinitarian doctrine, and especially on the question of the relation of the Son to the Father, is evidence of the centrality of this issue for the whole Christian witness to the pagan world of that time.

By contrast, during the era of 'Christendom' the doctrine of the Trinity has not occupied a comparable place in the thought of Christians. Not that there has been any widespread tendency among devout Christians to deny the doctrine, but simply that it has usually been regarded as a venerable formulation handed down from the past, or perhaps—if we are in an apologetic situation—a troublesome piece of theological baggage which is best kept out of sight when trying to commend the faith to unbelievers. It is significant that during the great theological struggle to the Reformation, the doctrine of the Trinity was never in dispute.

But it is also significant that, when one goes outside the 'Christendom' situation to bring the Gospel to non-Christians, one soon discovers that the doctrine of the Trinity is not something that can be kept out of sight; on the contrary, it is the necessary starting point of preaching. Even in the simplest form of missionary preaching, one finds that one cannot escape dealing with this doctrine. When an evangelist goes into an Indian village where the name of Jesus is unknown and preaches the Gospel for the first time, how is he to introduce the Name? How does one say who Jesus is, in a pagan situation? Presumably the hearers have already the word 'god' in their vocabulary. How is the name of Jesus to be related henceforth in their minds to that word? I have sometimes heard the Gospel preached in such a way that the hearers—accustomed to many gods—were led to think that the name of Jesus represented yet another god, this time more powerful and beneficent than those they already knew. Clearly that would not be the Christian faith as the New Testament understands it. I have always found, in talking to such village groups, that they had already in their minds the consciousness, however vague, of one God behind all the gods, One who was their creator and judge. If this consciousness is present, how does one relate the name of Jesus to it? Does one say that 'Jesus' is the name of that one God? Clearly, again, this would not be the New Testament faith. The truth is that one cannot preach Jesus even in the simplest terms without preaching him as the Son. His revelation of God is the revelation of 'an only begotten from the Father', and you cannot preach him without speaking of the Father and the Son.

Moreover, if the evangelist is wise, he will take time to listen before he talks. And if he does so, he will probably find that things have happened in the experience of his hearers which—without any human planning—have prepared the way for them to receive the Gospel. A time will come when they will look back upon these things as Christians and will recognize them as the prevenient work of the Spirit, the same Spirit who spoke to them in the preaching of the evangelist, the same Spirit who enabled them to receive the human words of the Evangelist as the Word of God. The true evangelist knows that the faith of these new Christians is not the effect of which his words were the cause; he knows that his words were but instruments of the work of the Spirit, a work which began before he arrived and continues after he left, of which their faith is the fruit.

Thus even in its most elementary form the preaching of the Gospel must presuppose an understanding of the triune nature of God. It is not, as we have sometimes seemed to say, a kind of intellectual cap-stone which can be put on to the top of the arch at the very end; it is, on the contrary, what Athanasius called it, the *arche*, the presupposition without which the preaching of the Gospel in a pagan world cannot begin.

This is not to suggest that an explicit trinitarian theology will be the substance either of the preacher's talk or of the new converts' understanding. We have already said that even in the New Testament itself such an explicit trinitarian theology is not found. But it is to say that a true understanding of the questions which God raises for us in our time, and a true restatement of the meaning of the missionary task will rest, as the New Testament rests, upon the revelation of God as Father, Son and Spirit.

It will be the purpose of the following paragraphs to seek to justify this thesis by looking at the three questions formulated earlier in the light of the trinitarian faith. At this stage it may perhaps be accepted as at least a reasonable suggestion that a fresh articulation of the meaning of the missionary task in terms of the pluralistic, polytheistic, pagan society of our time may require us likewise to acknowledge the necessity of a trinitarian starting point.

V: Missions and the Shape of World History

We turn, then, to the three issues which we have suggested as illustrations of the grounds for hesitancy in the work of missions. The first concerns the relation between the work of missions and what we may expect to happen in history. We have seen that this is an urgent question, and we have seen that in the recent past it has been answered in two principal ways. On the one hand missions have been seen as forwarding and completing the natural evolution of human society. The 'Christianization of the world' has been understood as something substantially continuous with the general progress of human development. On the other hand, and in sharp reaction to this, it has been insisted that the Gospel is radically other than all natural human religion and culture and that the mission of the Church is therefore something other than a mere reinforcement or prolongation of the natural course of human progress. We have seen also that this necessary and proper reminder has created a situation in which missions have been in danger of proceeding as though they were concerned only with the development of the Churches, as though the events of secular history were merely the background for the working out of God's plan of salvation, and not part of the plan itself. We are now in a situation where it becomes urgently necessary to ask: What is the relation between what God has done once for all in Christ and is continuing to do through the witness of the Church, and the events of world history as a whole? Does the trinitarian starting point help us to face this decisive question?

38

The Gospel records, and the New Testament as a whole, show us Jesus as the Son of the Father, as the 'Beloved Son', as the 'Only begotten from the Father'. It is impossible to think of him or to speak of him truly apart from the Father. He reveals God by showing us the love and obedience of the Son to the Father. No account of the Gospel which does not put this in the centre can be accepted.

God's fatherly rule of all things is at the very heart of his teaching. God sustains all, cares for all, rules over all. Even in the most strongly apocalyptic passages this note continues to sound: 'The end is not yet.' God in his mercy still gives time, still maintains the world in being, in order that there may be time for repentance. This is in line with biblical teaching as a whole. God who created all things, also sustains them and directs them according to his will. Even the great pagan political powers are in his hands to be used for his fatherly purposes, whether of chastisement (Assyria) or of help (Cyrus). Neither imperialism nor anti-imperialism is a mere work of the devil: God rules and uses them all.

As the Son, Jesus loves and obeys the Father. He submits himself wholly to the Father's ordering of events. He does not seek to take control himself of world history. He rejects every temptation to become himself a ruler and director of events. He does not appear among men as a theophany, in the sense of a temporary manifestation of the Ruler of all things; he appears as the Son who lovingly submits himself to the will of him who rules all things. Nor does he seek to launch a movement which will have power to control world events. When his disciples seek to take such power into their own hands he rebukes them. He warns them that they cannot expect power and influence. From first to last he accepts the Father's ordering of events as the form in which his mission, and that of his followers, is to be fulfilled.

Nevertheless his coming is the decisive event for mankind—for all men and for all history. In him the Kingdom of God has come, but it is hidden. His coming therefore means both salvation and judgment for the world, because by their acceptance or rejection of him men are judged. His coming is not merely the launching of a religious movement. He does not send out his disciples merely to spread a doctrine or a programme. He sends them out as witnesses to men of the fact that the decisive event of all history has arrived and is impending. But this event is not one of which he is in control. The Father alone is in control. Yet the coming of the Son is the event by which the Father has chosen to bring all things to the point of decision, to the issue of judgment and salvation. And this event is—so to say—extended in the mission of the disciples sent out before the crucifixion and of the apostles sent out after the resurrection. In these events the Father is bringing human history to its decisive moment—like a householder calling his servants to the reckoning, or the farmer setting out to reap his field.

Thus the Son and those whom he has made his brethren are sent into the world not as the agents of the Father's rule, but as the witnesses of it; by his coming, and by their going in his Name, the Father calls human history to its final issues. But this is not otherwise than by the presence of God's Spirit himself. It is when he sees the Spirit descending as a dove that Jesus also hears the voice, 'Thou art my beloved Son.' It is as one anointed by the Spirit that he stands up in the synagogue at Capernaum to announce the year of the Lord's favour. And it is not blasphemy against the Son, but blasphemy against the Spirit speaking and working in him that becomes the occasion for final condemnation. Likewise for the disciples also, it is the Spirit who is the witness. It is by his presence that they receive the gift of sonship and are enabled thereby to continue in the world the ministry of the Son. It is the Spirit who is the earnest of their inheritance, the instalment and proof of the glorious end to which history is being brought by the Father; and therefore it is the Spirit himself, rather than the disciples, who is the witness of that which the Father is doing. It is he who speaks when the persecuted disciples are on trial. It is he who convicts the world of sin, righteousness and judgment—that world which hates and rejects Jesus. It is he who is, properly speaking, the missionary.

Thus the Christian mission is the clue to world history, not in the sense that it is the 'winning side' in the battle with the other forces of human history, but in the sense that it is the point at which the meaning of history is understood and at which men are required to make the final decisions about that meaning. It is, so to say, not the motor but the blade, not the driving force but the cutting edge. Christians do not go through the battles of history as the master race. They go through them as the servant people, looking up to the Father who is alone the Lord of history, accepting his disposition of events as the context of their obedience, relying on his Spirit as their guide. They go through history as the witness people, in whom the Spirit is present to bear witness of the real meaning of the things which happen in the world, so that—*in relation to these things*—men are compelled to make decisions for or against God.

The most sustained and explicit New Testament statements of the relation between the mission of the Church and events of world history are to be found in the apocalyptic sections of the first three Gospels and in the discourses at the end of the fourth Gospel. In both the synoptic and Johannine discourses certain notes are repeated—hatred of the world against the Church, the rejection of Christ by the world, the tribulation of the Church in the world, the presence of the Spirit who answers the accusations of the world, the victory of Christ. It will be helpful to look in a little more detail at the discourse attributed to our Lord in Mark 13 as an answer to the enquiries of the disciples about the things to come.

The discourse is placed in the context of the question about the Temple. The disciples had been marvelling at its splendours. The Lord answers with a prophecy of its utter destruction. There could not have been any prophecy which more completely negated the hopes of loyal Israelites for the coming of God's Kingdom. Mount Zion was the place to which, according to Isaiah, the nations of the earth would come to acknowledge the Lord as the source of justice and peace.

The disciples, naturally shocked and perplexed, asked for an interpretation of what is to come. The answer which they received has at least the following elements relevant to our present discussion.

(*a*) 'Many will come in my name, saying, "I am he!" and they will lead many astray.' That is to say, there will be false Christs, those who falsely claim to bring what only the true Messiah can bring. This is not a warning against the powers of evil in general, it is far more specific. It is a warning against that particular form of evil that is possible only in a context in which the Christ is known or expected. It is a warning against the false Christs, ultimately against the antichrist.

The need for this warning arises from the nature of God's revelation in Christ. His coming into the world brings men face to face with their final destiny. The possibilities which are opened up for men by his coming are the possibilities of total salvation and of total loss. In his presence neutrality is ultimately impossible. Men are driven, gently but inexorably, to the point where they must either acknowledge him as Lord or denounce him as an impostor. In the fourth Gospel this is expressed by means of the symbolism of light and darkness. He is the light of the world, the true light, the only light that men have. By his coming men are compelled either to accept the light in its fullness, or else to walk in darkness. Therefore his coming means judgment, separation, polarization. In the fourth Gospel this is most graphically shown in the story of Judas, who in the end separates himself finally from Christ and his people and goes out deliberately into the darkness.

Both the discourses of John 14–16, and the apocalyptic passages such as the one we are studying, project this process of polarization prophetically through history. It does not stop with the end of Jesus' earthly ministry. It is extended through time, by the witness of the Church. And it is in this context that we are to understand the warning against false 'Christs', who offer men salvation on other terms than those which God has offered to mankind in Jesus. The offer of the false Christs can be made only in a context in which God's gift of salvation in Jesus had been made.

Thus it is entirely in accordance with what the New Testament would lead us to expect that the present era, in which for the first time the Christian message (in however diluted a form) has penetrated into every part of the world, should also be a time in which messianic movements of all kinds arise. The greater part of the human race has lived until relatively recent times without belief in the possibility of a total salvation, in the sense in which the New Testament portrays it. There has been indeed belief in the possibility of salvation for the individual by withdrawal from involvement in the affairs of the world, but there has not been belief in the possibility of a corporate salvation for mankind as the goal to which human affairs move. This is a new and revolutionary belief. The effect of it is to disrupt for ever the ancient cyclical conceptions of time in which the majority of men have lived, and to set men thinking in linear terms—in terms of advance towards some kind of new order in the future.

The revolutionary character of our time arises from the fact that whole peoples who have lived for millennia without the expectation that human life would ever be radically different from what it has been are now persuaded of the possibility of a wholly new order of existence. The content given to this vision of a new order varies; but the form of the hope is recognizably the same everywhere. It has not arisen from any of the ancient non-Christian systems of thought. It has arisen from the contact of these systems with the impulses that have come from a culture shaped by the biblical understanding of the meaning of history. In fact it is this hope of a new order which gives to Western culture its driving power and enables it to disrupt such ancient and stable human structures as the civilization of India and China. It is a striking fact, as Christopher Dawson has pointed out, that the movements which have been successful in enabling the former colonies to throw off the political yoke of the colonial powers have been themselves movements dependent upon the West for their ideological basis. Movements—such as the Hindu Maha Sabha in India, and the Muslim Brotherhood in Egypt—which sought their ideological basis in the ancient non-Christian faiths have not succeeded in capturing the political leadership of the anti-colonial movement. The revolutionary movements of our time, even though predominantly anti-Western in their political orientation, are movements which would be inconceivable as products of the ancient religions of Asia or Africa. They are powered by a variety of secularized forms of the biblical hope of the Kingdom of God. Essentially they are messianic movements. They cannot be understood in the categories of the non-biblical religions.

Such movements are potentially bearers both of good and of evil. They have been and are—even in their militantly anti-Christian forms—means of liberation for millions from injustice and bondage, bearers of new intellectual and spiritual life, instruments of awakening to new truth and new concern. They bring gifts which are God's gifts. Yet in so far as they claim to offer total welfare to men, and claim therefore men's total allegiance, they become bearers of evils ultimately more fearful than those from which they liberated men. If we have understood the passage we are studying, this is what we should expect. The coming of the true Messiah leads to the appearing of the false ones. The coming of him who is the true End of history— the Omega as he is the Alpha—precipitates the necessity for decision, and forces men out of the cyclical understanding of time in which no decisions are final. The offer of God's salvation precipitates the offers of salvation (total welfare for mankind) on other terms than God's. This is part of that polarization of human affairs which begins with the coming of the Word made flesh. It does not mean that God's cause has suffered a defeat; it is among the things which 'must come to pass'. It is part of the price God is willing to pay for man's salvation.

Here one must enter a word of caution. To say that these revolutionary movements are to be understood in the terms of this chapter does not mean that any one of them is to be identified as the antichrist. This discourse itself, which is a summons to recognize the signs of the times and to interpret the events of human history in the light of God's work in Christ, also contains a warning against the error of identifying a particular event with the ultimate event. But 'of that day or that hour no one knows, not even the angels in heaven, nor the Son, but only the Father.[1] We are not permitted to know what are the limits of God's patience, or the bounds which he has set for human history. But we are obliged to recognize in these movements a conscious answer to a question which—apart from Christ—has not been posed, the question of salvation for mankind, an answer which is therefore post-Christian and anti-Christian in a sense in which paganism is not. They are movements, therefore, orientated towards the issue which Christ raises for mankind, and this fact determines the duty of the Church in relation to them. That duty is indicated in the next section of Mark 13.

(*b*) 'But take heed to yourselves; for they will deliver you up to councils; and you will be beaten in synagogues; and you will stand before governors and kings for my sake, to bear testimony before them. And the gospel must first be preached to all nations.' The task of the Church in relation to the events of world history is not to be the governor and controller of them, but to be the suffering servant and witness of the Lord, manifesting in its witness the true meaning of these events. The Church is not the instrument of God's governance of the world, but the witness of his governance both by speaking and by suffering.

The closeness of our missionary thinking to the New Testament may perhaps be in part judged by the place which we accord to suffering in our understanding of the calling of the Church. During the long centuries of the 'Constantinian era' of Church history, when Christians have normally had the authority of the state behind them, it has been regarded as abnormal that Christians should suffer for their faith. Even when modern

---

1. If, as seems possible, the differences between Mark 13 : 14–23 and Luke 21 : 20–24 are the result of a rewriting of the Marcan material in the light of the events of AD70, this establishes still more clearly the same point. The New Testament interpretation of the events of history in terms of apocalyptic does *not* imply either that particular events are identified with the end, or that particular persons are identified with antichrist.

missions went out into the non-Christian cultures of Asia, Africa, America and the Pacific, they had behind them the power of the European nations, and they often expected to be protected by it. As the result of this long experience, many Christians seem to take it for granted that the 'normal' state of affairs, which one ought to be able to expect, is that one can go anywhere and preach Christianity—or indeed any other religion—and be protected by the forces of law and order in doing so. This is a mirage for which neither Scripture nor common sense provides any foundation. No human societies cohere except on the basis of some kind of common beliefs and customs. No society can permit these beliefs and practices to be threatened beyond a certain point without reacting in self-defence. The idea that we ought to be able to expect some kind of neutral secular political order, which presupposes no religious or ideological beliefs, and which holds the ring impartially for a plurality of religions to compete with one another, has no adequate foundation. The New Testament makes it plain that Christ's followers must expect suffering as the normal badge of their discipleship, and also as one of the characteristic forms of their witness.

This does not, however, mean that the Church is to play a merely passive rôle in relation to the events of the world. Christians are called, with their Lord, both to preach and to act. The preaching of the Gospel to the whole world is the witness to the cosmic nature of what God has done in Christ. It is the witness to the fact that 'what Jesus began to do and to teach' was not just one of the strands that make up human history, but was the disclosing of the true end of that history. This is why the disciples are bidden to hurry on without waiting to argue with those who reject the announcement that the Kingdom of God has drawn near. This is why St Paul hurries to the farthest West without waiting to build on the foundations which he had laid in the eastern lands of the Roman world. This is why foreign missions have an abiding significance which is not exhausted by the concept of universal church extension. It is of the essence of the specifically missionary task that it involves crossing over into another human situation, in which the Gospel has to be articulated in terms of that situation. This readiness to relate the Gospel with constantly new human situations is an essential part of the Church's witness to the character of what God has done for all men in Christ. Without this, the Gospel becomes too easily denatured by a process of domestication. The phrase 'all the nations' has to be taken seriously, and for this reason the phrase 'foreign missions' still has its own propriety and necessity. Naturally, however, the biblical word translated 'nation' is not to be simply identified with the particular kind of human group which is described by that word in modern English.

And Christians are called also to act. In this they are one with their Lord, who was anointed both to announce good news and also to embody that good news in acts of healing, releasing, quickening. These acts will also have the character of witness. They will be signs rather than instruments. This is true of the older forms of service in institutions of teaching and healing, and in the newer programmes of technical aid. These signs may be— like the loaves and the fishes—misinterpreted. They may be made the occasion for perverted forms of messianism (see Jn. 6:15). These perverted forms of messianism appear even within the Christian fellowship—a fact which should be pondered by Christians who interpret other movements in terms of messianism. The works which are properly understood as signs of the Kingdom may become themselves the objects of men's desire, and so cause a rejection of Jesus' own claim (Jn. 6:41ff.) and even the falling away of his disciples (Jn. 6:60–66). Yet properly understood they are a necessary part of the Church's witness to the presence and power of God's Kingdom. They are not the *means* by which God establishes his Kingdom. They are the witnesses to its present reality. The Church is not required (as speakers sometimes suggest) to try to control or overcome the revolutionary movements of our time. These movements are themselves inexplicable apart from the impact of ideas and ways of life derived from the Bible upon the peoples of the world. The Church is rather called to be present everywhere within these movements as the witnessing, suffering servant of God, believing in his sovereign rule and becoming the place where that rule is made manifest, the place, therefore, where men are called upon to decide for or against God.

(c) But this witness is not a work of the Church. It is the work of the Holy Spirit dwelling with the Church. 'And when they bring you to trial and deliver you up, do not be anxious beforehand what you are to say; but say whatever is given you in that hour, for it is not you who speak, but the Holy Spirit.' Similarly in the Johannine discourses it is said that when the Spirit comes he will convince the world of sin, of righteousness and of judgment. The witness which the Church bears to the world is thus not something contrived by the Church itself. It is the work of the triune God. The occasions for it are ordained by the Father in whose ordering of all things it is permitted that Christians should be brought into suffering and rejection. The substance of it is the work of the Holy Spirit who, in his sovereign freedom, uses the occasions of the Church's weakness and trouble to speak his own convincing word to the world. Christians are called thus to continue through history the ministry of Christ, looking up to the Father as those who share his Sonship, accepting the Father's disposition of events as the form in which their mission is to be accomplished, rejoicing in the presence of the Spirit who gives them the foretaste of God's completed purpose and therefore confronts the world with the most powerful witness to that purpose and with the necessity to accept or reject it.

Thus the Church can make her own the words of the great missionary apostle: 'But thanks be to God, who in Christ always leads us in triumph, and through us spreads the fragrance of the knowledge of him everywhere. For we are the aroma of Christ to God among those who are being saved and among those who are perishing, to one a fragrance from death to death, to the other a fragrance from life to life,' (2 Cor. 2:14–15). It ought not to surprise us if we find that the penetration of the Gospel, and of ideas and ways of life shaped by the Bible, into all parts of the world, has been followed both by the creation of living Christian communities *and* by the rise of messianic movements which claim to offer salvation to the nations on other terms. This is simply the continuing of that which God began to do in Jesus, the confronting of the nations in ever sharper terms with the choice between the true purpose of the Father to sum up all things in him through whom they were created, and the sub-stitutes for that purpose which are offered by those who falsely claim to bring total welfare to men. It is the Father's purpose, revealed in Jesus, to lead all mankind to this ultimate decision. The presence of the Church in the midst of mankind is the means by which he does so. But the witness to his purpose which brings men to the point of decision is the witness of the Holy Spirit himself. Precisely in the midst of opposition and rejection the Church can say: 'Thanks be to God who, in Christ, always leads us in triumph.'

It is worthwhile adding that this understanding of the relation of the Christian mission to world history has a close relevance to the question of the meeting of the Gospel with the non-Chris-tian religions. In their present form these religions must be understood as post-Christian phenomena. Their present signs of renaissance are their response to the impact upon them of all the spiritual forces that have come from contact with the Western world. Their leaders are wrestling with the problems raised by the impact of the dynamic society of the West upon the relatively static societies of Asia and Africa. For the most part they are eager to explore and make their own the scientific ideas of the Western world, but are uninterested in the biblical roots of Western thought.

If Christians are to bear witness to Christ in their contact with the modern representatives of these great religions, they must be able to interpret the source and character of this dynamic society which is becoming the common society of mankind. They must be able to show how it raises issues which have not been raised in the ancient non-Christian religions, and how it must disrupt the ancient cyclical understanding of human life and raise new questions concerning the nature and destiny of man, questions which ultimately lead to the question of Jesus Christ himself. Such matters of urgent concern to the nations of Asia and Africa as the nature and limitation of planning, the idea of the secular state, the character and purpose of education, the place of the family in society, are matters on which Christians ought to be able to bear witness to the meaning of what God is doing with mankind through Christ.

But this witness will occur only if it is, so to say, not the contrived witness of the Church, but the sovereign activity of the Spirit dwelling in the Church. It may be in a quite unexpected way and from a quite unexpected quarter that the Spirit will bear witness, using perhaps some small piece of simple fidelity, or some unstudied word, to illuminate with the authority of light itself what the Church has been trying to say about the purpose of God. The Church must therefore not be anxious how or what to say, but be anxious rather that all her life, even in the seemingly unimportant details, is open to the sovereign government of the Holy Spirit of God.

(*d*) Finally, the whole thirteenth chapter of St Mark is dominated by the assurance that God is leading all things to a final consummation in which the powers of antichrist will muster all their strength against the Kingdom of God and will be finally vanquished. The process of polarization goes on to the end. The conflict grows more acute, the decisions become more urgent. There is no gradual ascent to a perfect world. World history does not contain in itself the secret of its own redemption. The Church, which is embedded in world history, belongs to it, and bears witness to its true beginning and end, is nevertheless apart from world history, in the sense that its witness is to an end which is not merely implicit in the story itself. The relation of the Church to man in his history is, therefore, not merely one of solidarity, but also one of separation. Here also the Church, when it is faithful, follows the Lord who by his very solidarity with men pronounced the divine judgment on them, whose Cross was both the ultimate sign of his complete identification with sinful men and also the point at which God's total rejection of man's sin was manifested. Perhaps this double character is expressed in his preference for the mysterious title 'Son of Man', which could mean both 'man' in the simplest sense and also the mysterious supernatural figure whom Daniel saw coming with the clouds of heaven.

The foregoing paragraphs do not pretend to do justice to the whole breadth of the biblical teaching about the relation of the Christian missions to world history. But reflection on this chapter can perhaps put us into a position where we can hear what the Bible has to say on the question with which we began. Not that the Bible ever answers our questions exactly in the form in which we put them. The Bible always requires of us a shift in standpoint, for which time and patience are needed. Our thesis is that from the standpoint of this chapter we can begin to understand the coherence and the relevance of the trinitarian faith as it illuminates the questions we are asking: in what sense is God at work in secular history? And how is the missionary work of the Church related to God's work in secular history?

Negatively, the biblical standpoint excludes certain assumptions which are often present, unexamined, in our minds. Firstly, the old pagan picture of history as a conflict between 'virtue' and 'fate', as a struggle between the spirit of man (aided, doubtless, by the divine spirit) and the forces of the environment, has to be rejected. It is the very heart of the trinitarian faith that the same God who is manifest in Jesus Christ, and who is known in the presence of the Spirit in our hearts, is the God who created and rules the whole frame of things and events. Secondly, the Bible gives us no ground for the idea that the world as a whole, by a process of gradual improvement, is going to become more 'Christ-like', and no ground for thinking, therefore, that the work of Christian missions will be found to be, in this sense, going 'with the stream'. Thirdly, the Bible knows of no other saving name than that of Jesus Christ. However God may direct and use the forces of secular history, these forces do not contain any alternative or supplementary way of salvation. God's purpose for the world proceeds by the way of election, of choosing; and the Chosen and Beloved is none other than Jesus Christ.

Positively the heart of the biblical teaching concerning the questions we are asking is that Jesus Christ is the beginning and the end of all things, that his coming into the midst of history is the revelation of its end, and that this coming therefore precipitates a double process of gathering and separating, of consummation and judgment. The mission of the Church in the world is the continuation of that double process through history till its end. Missions, in the sense of a particular kind of action within the total mission of the Church, are the means by which new human communities are brought within the range of this process.

But these bald statements cannot be properly understood except in the context of the full statement concerning who Jesus is—that is to say, in the context of the trinitarian faith. Jesus is the Son of the Father. It is the Father alone who knows the times and seasons, and who determines them. It is he who sent the Son when the time for sending was ripe. It is he who over-rules the events of human history in such wise that they converge upon Jesus Christ. The Church which is sent forth in his name, and as the continuance of his sending, does not go out into an alien world simply to propagate its own convictions. It goes out into a world which belongs to and is ruled by the Father of the Lord Jesus Christ, and in proclaiming him it announces to that world its true end. Thereby it constantly repeats in its own life the experience of the Lord. Just as his coming precipitated both a gathering and a separation, both the discipleship of Peter and the enmity of Caiaphas, so in the mission of the Church there is a like double experience. But this experience is all over-ruled by the Father. It is he who preserves the world in sufficient stability and order for human life to continue, who provides rain both for the just and for the unjust, who allows both wheat and tares to grow together till the harvest, who preserves—in short—sufficient human freedom to enable men to accept Jesus as their Lord, or to reject him. And it is likewise he who so rules the currents of history that men are brought to this choice, that even in spite of the faithlessness and apostasy of the Church, the very events of secular history drive men to the final issues of human existence, to the question of the true Omega, and therefore to the question of Christ—or antichrist. The Father rules all things and works through whatever way he chooses. He is not confined to the Church. He can and does use what and whom he will to serve him. But his working has a visible centre and point of reference. Jesus Christ, the God-Man, eternal and yet part of history, is the Omega; it is in his coming in the flesh, as a man of a certain place and time, that the ultimate issues are posed for men. And it is in his continuing coming to men through the missionary work of the Church that these issues are posed ever afresh for men's conscious and deliberate acceptance or rejection.

But this 'continuing coming' is not simply an enterprise of the Church. It is the work of the living Spirit of God, of him who is one with the Father and the Son. The Church is the outward form of the continuous work of the Spirit in re-enacting Christ's coming among men. It is by the presence of the Spirit that men are enabled to confess Jesus as Lord, and thereby to know the sovereign ruler of all events as Father. The Spirit is the earnest of the fulfilment of God's purpose; in him we have the foretaste of the consummation of all things in Christ. By him we are enabled to live in confident hope of that consummation, and to act also in the assurance that it will be as we hope. Those who so live and act become witnesses—even by their unguarded words and deeds—of the consummation in the hope of which they live. This witness is not primarily a matter of 'religious' language, but concerns the whole secular life of mankind, because it is witness to God's intention to 'sum it all up' in the glorified humanity of Jesus Christ. Where the Spirit rules, words and actions bear witness to the hidden and hoped for reign of Christ in the terms of the ordinary affairs of secular history—because the Spirit is one with the Father who rules all things, and with the Son in whom all things are to be consummated.

The Spirit who thus bears witness in the life of the Church to the purpose of the Father is not confined within the limits of the Church. It is the clear teaching of the Acts of the Apostles, as it is the experience of missionaries, that the Spirit goes, so to speak, ahead of the Church. Like Cornelius, men of every age and nation have been miraculously prepared beforehand to receive the message of Christ. But—because the Spirit and the

Father are one—this work of the Spirit is not in any sense an alternative way to God apart from the Church; it is the preparation for the coming of the Church, which means that the Church must be ever ready to follow where the Spirit leads.

Similarly the divine over-ruling by which the Father governs all things and directs them to their true end is something far beyond either the activity or even the understanding of the Church. Yet, because the Father is one with the Son and with the Spirit, this divine governance of events is not something apart from, or alternative to, what God is doing in the Church. It has the double character already alluded to: it both preserves an area of freedom wherein men may live and make their decisions, and it leads men to the decision concerning their final destiny. It is not confined to the work of the Church, but it is not detached from it, for its ultimate purpose is to lead men to the acceptance of their true destiny in Christ.

We may sum this up by saying that the Church's mission to all the nations is a participation in the work of the triune God. In it, Christ continues his work of confronting men with the decision concerning their true end. It becomes, as he was in his incarnate life, the point at which the end becomes immediate for men; the Kingdom of God is at hand. But the mission is fulfilled, as his ministry was fulfilled, in dependence upon the Father who determines the events by which it is outwardly governed, and who alone knows and determines the times of growing and of harvest. The outward circumstances which govern it may—and certainly will—include suffering, defeat, apostasy, the rise of false messianic claims. Success is not measured by the number of adherents or the range of visible influence upon affairs. The significance of the Church's missionary witness will lie at this point: that it is the place where men are confronted with the reality and power of God's Kingdom. The rest is in the hands of the Father. It is sufficient for the Church that it be faithful. But this is not to be a matter of anxiety. The witness to the Kingdom is not the work of men but of the Spirit. The mission of God is not to be prosecuted after the manner of a human crusade. It is the participation of the Church in the Spirit's witness to what the Father is doing with the whole maze of events which make up human life—namely to sum up all things in Christ, in whom they were all created.

Such a faith gives us a place for free, responsible action. It gives the assurance that what we do is not lost in the abyss of meaninglessness, but is part of the fulfilling of God's purpose for history. It delivers us on the one hand from the alternations of optimism and pessimism which beset any undertaking not rooted in faith concerning God's whole action in history. It delivers us on the other hand from the kind of over-heated apocalypticism which is not content to leave 'the day and the hour' in the Father's hands. In this faith we can go out into every nation to preach Christ as Lord, knowing that, whatever be the result, we are thereby sharing in the work of God and shall share in his joy.

VI: Missions and the Secularization of Human Life

The second factor which we suggested as a ground for perplexity in the work of Christian missions is the increasing secularization of human life, the withdrawal of more and more areas of human experience from direct reference to religion.

In spite of the fact that this process of secularization was already well-established in Europe in the eighteenth century, the missionaries of that and the succeeding centuries still had a great deal of the mental attitude of a religiously centred society. They came from towns and villages in which the churches were the most notable buildings and from nations in which, for most part, the Church held a central place in public life, in works of teaching, healing and philanthropy, and in 'the cure of souls'. What is still more important, they came to societies which were for the most part thoroughly 'sacral' in their structure; that is to say, in which religion held a controlling position in the affairs of the community and the family. It was therefore only natural that the new Christian communities which grew up around the person of the missionary had a similarly 'sacral' character. Where, as in some of the Pacific Islands, the whole community accepted Christianity, the sacral character of the whole community continued without rupture. The new religion became the effective bond of the old society. Where, as in India, only a minority accepted the Christian faith, it was nevertheless true that the Christian community and the institutions of the Church were largely conformed to the pattern of a 'sacral' society. The Church conducted schools, hospitals and institutions of social service, and involved itself directly in the conduct of industries, the improvement of agriculture, and the general organization of society. Within the frontiers of the Christian community the missionary and the pastor had many of the functions of the magistrate. The Church, even in the twentieth century, had a position of centrality in the life of the community which it had long since lost in the majority of the countries from which the missionaries came.

In most parts of the world this situation is changing rapidly. The educational and social services which the Church began are taken over by the state. The old forms of ecclesiastical discipline are no longer accepted. The old village community, centred in the church, gives place to the new town, dominated by the factory, in which the church appears to represent only the private and spare-time interest of a minority. The process of secularization goes forward relentlessly in every part of the world.

From one point of view one can describe this process as a growing liberation of the individual from the control of the national communities of family and locality. In the old type of village community men are confined to the society of their neighbours and they have no choice of friends. In a modern city, aided by a car or telephone, a man can ignore his neighbours and choose his friends at will. He is thus free, in large measure, to choose the standards under which he will live. Nothing is, in quite the old sense, given. The same freedom extends to other areas of life. The form of government under which he will live is not something simply given, it is chosen. The way in which one earns one's living is, in a modern society, a matter of personal choice to a degree undreamed of in older societies. Money is no longer a fixed standard, related finally to the value of gold or silver, by which the values of things may be compared; it is a flexible instrument manipulated by governments to control economic development. Less and less is mankind compelled to accept the facts of social, political and economic life as given: more and more are they matters for deliberate decision. This extends from the most intimate matters of personal and family

life to the widest questions concerning the life of man in
society.

Since from one point of view this dissolution of the 'given' is
a liberating process, it is quite futile for the Church to regret it,
even when it means that old social solidarities are dissolved. This
dissolution may be painful—as when an African pastor sees his
village congregation eroded by forces coming from the mines
and the big cities: or when the elders of an island community in
the South Pacific witness the shattering impact upon their
people of the tourist invasion. The Church may, and indeed
must, do what it can to mitigate for the sake of the human beings
involved, the immediate effect of the inrush of these new forces
into old communities. But it is clear that in the long run the old
kind of sacral community cannot be preserved. The challenge of
man's coming of age has to be accepted. Christian faith and
discipleship will be more and more a matter of personal decision: less and less will it be possible to hold men to that faith by
the bonds of custom and the sanctions of social pressure. There
may still be room, among relatively primitive peoples, for group
movements into the Church such as have characterized most of
the story of missions through the centuries, but it will surely be
a diminishing place. Likewise also the place of direct ecclesiastical action and influence in the fields of education, medicine
and social service will surely be a diminishing one, as these areas
of life become increasingly secularized. The Christian teacher,
the Christian doctor and the Christian social worker will increasingly have to work—like the Christian merchant, manufacturer
or engineer—without the protection of a 'Christian institution'
around him.

What has been said in the previous section concerning the
Church as the place where God presses mankind towards decision for or against Christ should prepare us to recognize the
development we are now considering. It ought not to find
Christians perplexed or unready. In fact it is precisely the work
of Christian missions which has been the great instrument of
secularization in the midst of the ancient religious societies of
Asia and Africa. The preaching of Jesus Christ as the sole

Redeemer, liberating men from the hitherto unbreakable grip of the old sacral order in family and tribe, has been itself the great revolutionary force. At this point the experience of Asian and African Christians, for whom secularization means first of all a kind of liberation, can be a help to the Christians of Europe for whom secularization appears as a wholly menacing reality, threatening the last remains of the sacral society of Christendom.

But, if we have to be on our guard against the typical religious illusion that the forms of Christian 'sacral' society can be indefinitely preserved, we have also to keep ourselves free from the typically secularist illusion that liberation from the 'given' means that human freedom is secured. There is no such security. The liberation contains indeed the possibility of freedom, but it is only in Christ that the possibility can be actualized. Without the deliberate acceptance of that service which is perfect freedom, secular man falls immediately into a new kind of bondage. It is precisely in those societies where the maximum of individual freedom has been achieved as part of the process of secularization that one finds also new forms of bondage to anonymous powers, 'economic forces', the 'hidden persuaders' and the rest. Nowhere is this more poignantly evident than in the fact that while millions of men passionately desire peace, they find themselves apparently driven by an almost impersonal fate towards war. It is only in the service of Christ that freedom is found; liberation from the 'given' is misunderstood and lost if it is not accepted as the opportunity for that service.

The fact that Christian faith and discipleship become more and more a matter of personal decision is fully in line with what we have understood of God's work in Christ. But it can also be misunderstood. The withdrawal of more and more areas of human life from the direct control of religion can be taken to mean that the Christian has nothing to say about them—that politics, economics, culture are not his concern. The fact that Christian faith becomes increasingly a matter of personal decision can be misunderstood to mean that Christianity is concerned only with the narrow range of personal moral problems.

When this happens, there is a grave danger that the Gospel may be mistaken for a mere offer of individual and private salvation, like the mystery religions which were its rivals during the first centuries of its mission. (There will always be an eager market for such religions!) The Gospel is concerned with something greater, with the redemption of the world, including precisely those realms of human life which are being so drastically secularized in our day. How are we to understand the secularization of these areas of human life in the light of a Gospel which announces their redemption? That is one of the burning practical issues for the Christian world mission today. How does the trinitarian faith help us to understand it?

The life of the incarnate Son of God, as shown to us in the Gospels, was a life lived in full acceptance of the human institutions of his time—political, social, economic. When St Peter writes: 'Be subject for the Lord's sake to every human institution,' he is faithfully reflecting the example of Jesus, who did not seek to overthrow or control the social structures under which he lived, though he was the emissary of a divine rule which in principle overturned them all, making the last first and the first last. He accepted them as part of the provision made by the Father for the preserving and ordering of human life. The primitive Church followed this example, apparently accepting such social and economic institutions as slavery and the subjection of women while yet proclaiming that in Christ there was neither male nor female, neither bond nor free. The same Paul who wrote 'Let every person be subject to the governing authorities. For there is no authority except from God,' also wrote that all 'dominions or principalities or authorities' were created through Christ and for Christ, and added 'He is before all things, and in him all things hold together.' These 'authorities' and 'institutions' were in no sense 'Christian'. The era of Constantine was still far in the future. Nevertheless they were to be acknowledged as God's creation through Christ and for Christ.

Christians have erred in two directions in seeking a right relation to these 'authorities' and 'institutions'. On the one hand they have sometimes forgotten that these things were created through Christ and for Christ and that they are therefore subject to his will. This has led to an absolutizing of certain forms of these institutions—such as slavery or personal monarchy—as unalterable parts of the created order at a time when the Spirit of God was moving Christians to find new forms for the economic and political ordering of human society. On the other hand Christians have sometimes forgotten that Jesus was subject to these institutions and that the Church is called to be, for his sake, subject to them also and not to seek to rule them. The best remembered example of this second error is the Hildebrandine Papacy, but there are others which could with more immediate profit be remembered, including some in the recent history of missions.

If the Churches are now forced to relinquish such direct control or influence as they have had in the recent past over the cultural and social life of mankind, this is not necessarily a defeat for the mission of the Church. It is a twofold reminder; negatively, of the fact that these spheres of life are indeed subject to Christ but not the Church, and that part of the Church's conformity to the will of her Lord lies in her accepting, like him, a certain subjection to the institutions which the Father has ordained for the safeguarding and ordering of human life. Positively, it is a reminder that Christ's lordship over these spheres of life is manifested not otherwise than by the work of the Holy Spirit, who is the earnest of our participation in his now hidden Lordship, and who takes of the things of Christ and shows them to us—not all at once, but as we are able to bear them. This positive point requires some further elaboration.

We have here to anticipate what will be said in the next section of this essay about the work of the Spirit in the Christian congregation. It is not the official organs of the Churches, their clergy, synods and 'church executives' who are in the closest daily contact with the institutions of political, economic and cultural life. It is the whole lay membership of the Churches, living and earning their daily bread in the business of politics, commerce, education, industry, scientific research and so on. It is by the decisions of these men and women, taken in the course of their week-day working lives, that these institutions of social life are changed—if they are changed at all. It is indeed possible—it happens all too often—that Christians working in these spheres behave as though they were completely outside the area of Christ's rule; as though their work in farm or factory from Monday to Friday were not 'the Lord's work' in the sense in which they apply that designation to their work in Sunday School or Bible class. That is, in effect, to deny Christ's cosmic Lordship. If we believe that all these spheres of human life, and all the 'principalities, dominions and authorities' which hold sway in them, were created through Christ and for Christ, then we shall expect that the Spirit who takes of the things of Christ and shows them to us, who is the foretaste of our share in his victory, will in his sovereign freedom lead men and women engaged in these secular tasks, singly or in groups, to specific acts which challenge the existing structures and witness to the true purpose for which God created them. The history of Christianity has many examples of such movements of the Spirit, sometimes resisted by the official authority of the Churches, by which the institutions of the state, economic life, education and law have been changed through the action of Christian men and women. But one has to confess with sorrow that these examples have been few in relation to the total involvement of Christians in the life of these institutions of human life in society.

It can certainly be said with thankfulness that the missionary record of the past two centuries is bright with the memory of successful battles in the name of Christ against social evil of all kinds. This is not the place to cite details. Two things are relevant here; first, that these achievements have been largely the work of the organized forces of the Churches, using the advantages which the power and prestige of the Western nations gave them, often against the forces of commerce and government; second, that with the changes now taking place in the world (to which missions have made a very large contribution) the place for this direct action of organized Churches and missions in the attack on social wrong is becoming much smaller. Secularization is everywhere the order of the day. Nostalgia for the days when Christian schools, hospitals and institutions of social service had unquestioned dominance in the field is of no avail. The call of this hour is to understand in depth the relation of the mission of the Church to the structures of social existence, such as state, industry, economic life and culture, and to draw the necessary consequences for practical action. It will already be clear that the essential elements of such an understanding will be something like the following:

(*a*) These structures are part of God's creation as the frame-work for human life. They are 'ordained by God'. The Church, following her Lord, has to accept them as the framework in which her life is to be lived, acknowledging them and fulfilling the specific duties which their proper character requires. They are not subject to the Church and are not to be directly controlled by ecclesiastical power. The obedience, which Christians render to the 'authorities' of—for example—the state, is part of their sharing in the obedience rendered by the Son to the Father. Thus even the obedience of a Christian slave to his master is commended by the example of him who 'When he was reviled, he did not revile in return; . . . but he trusted to him who judges justly.'

(*b*) Like all things created, they have been created through Christ and for Christ. They are to be summed up in Christ. This is therefore the norm by which they are to be interpreted. Yet, because of sin, they share in the corruption of the creation. They come under demonic powers which claim an absolute authority apart from Christ—the authority of 'reasons of state', 'economic necessity' and many others. When this happens they become the occasion for the enslaving and dehumanizing of man. The extreme example of this, so far as the New Testament is concerned, is the assumption of divine authority by the head of state. That which was 'ordained of God' then becomes 'the Beast'.

(*c*) Christ who, as the Son, humbled himself and became utterly subject to all the 'powers' for man's sake, has become victorious over all the demonic powers and has been exalted by the Father to his right hand until 'all things are put under his feet'. Both the past and the future tenses have to be taken seriously. His victory is complete; yet we await its completion. The creation still groans in bondage, waiting for its liberation. Demonic powers still work in the structures of human society. We do not yet see them manifestly subject to Christ, their rightful ruler. The Church has still to accept them as, even in their corrupted form, part of God's creation.

(*d*) But the Christ who sits at God's right hand till his enemies submit has not left us without a Comforter. The gift of the Spirit is the sign of Christ's victory. By sharing in the life of the Spirit, Christians share already in that victory and have therefore an unshakeable hope and assurance of it. It is in the light of that assurance that they see and judge the working of the 'structures' of society. By their sharing in the life of the Spirit they are able to confess Jesus as Lord of all these structures, and to acknowledge God as the Father who gave them to men to be their home, even though so much in them denies his Fatherhood. But this confession and acknowledgment do not remain a merely interior mental state. It breaks out into words and deeds, which the Spirit may use in his own freedom and sovereignty to bear witness to the Lordship of Christ over these structures of human life. This will not normally or primarily be a matter of the formal acts of the organized Churches—though these of course have their place within the administration of the Spirit. It will be more commonly the words and acts (perhaps casual and unpremeditated) of Christian men and women in the midst of their involvement in these 'structures'—as managers, technicians or labourers, as legislators, civil servants or voters, as teachers or students, as landowners or tenants or doctors or architects or journalists. It will be acts and words which arise within the workings of these structures, as Christian men and women, accepting the fundamental disciplines which these structures impose, wrestle with their problems in the assurance of Christ's Lordship and God's Fatherhood.

Yet not as isolated men and women. To say 'Christian men and women' is to speak of men and women knit together in the life of Christian congregations, sharing the common life which the Spirit gives, expressing it in worship and receiving it constantly afresh in the word and sacraments of the Gospel and the mutual help, counsel and admonition of the fellowship. It is a grave weakness of much of our congregational life that it does not appear to rest upon a serious belief in the authority and freedom of the Holy Spirit—his freedom to give gifts of discernment and leadership to any member of the fellowship which may be used for the strengthening and guiding of the rest; and his authority to determine the real strategy of the Christian mission—opening up lines of advance at points where we did not expect them, using the witness of those whom we had held of little account, sometimes closing doors that seemed open and full of promise. This point is stressed here, because it is surely only by learning what this authority and freedom of the Spirit mean in the life of a congregation that we shall go on to learn to trust and follow him in the formidable tasks of Christian witness in the world of politics, industry and culture.

The stress must fall first on the local congregation, because this is the point at which men learn to live together as neighbours, in which the neighbour becomes—in Christ—the brother. But in relation to the specific questions with which this section deals, it may be that free associations of Christian men and women working in the same field of secular life will prove of crucial significance for the future. The more that education in, for example, Asia and Africa is secularized and taken out of the hands of Churches, the more necessity will there be to provide opportunities for Christian teachers to share common membership in professional associations or orders in which they can seek together the guidance of the Spirit for their daily work. In areas where the Churches have not had, in the past, a comparable influence, such as industry or commerce, the need may be less acutely felt than it is by teachers: it is not less real and urgent.

There is a particular example of this need which is so important for the present phase of the world mission of the Church that special attention should be drawn to it. It is for a fellowship of Christian men and women who will accept the calling to a missionary penetration of the rapidly growing movements of international assistance for technical development. This would surely be the proper response of the Churches to the movement of secularization which is curtailing older forms of missionary outreach. It was suggested in some memorable sentences spoken by Canon Warren at the Willingen Meeting in 1952:

> . . . I believe there is a call for an entirely new type of missionary activity to be developed alongside the traditional modes. We need, for instance, to envisage men and women of scientific training who will be ready to give their service in development schemes, going to their work as ordinary salaried officials and bringing their expert knowledge to bear on come local situation. But they will go, not merely as those whose Christian convictions are marginal to their work, as is commonly the case of many today. Rather, they will go with a vocation consciously and deliberately to seek to work out 'a disciplined and purified technology' in the light of Christian insights. Promotion and financial reward will, by such men, be completely subordinated to their Christian vocation. Others with the same dedication will go as experienced trade unionists, to help ensure that the young trade union movements of Africa and Asia are built up on Christian insights as to the meaning of society and the responsibility of individuals to society and of society to individuals. Yet others will bring a Christian integrity to the development of co-operative movements. These are just three illustrations.
>
> I envisage the possibility of much a missionary brotherhood being pioneered by a number of men who would be banded together in a dedicated fellowship, with something of the same sense of cohesion and of spiritual support that has characterized the historic missionary societies. But I also dare to envisage something new. Such men will be going out into particular situations in what is largely unexplored territory. They will be often isolated and very much alone. They will need a very deep assurance of backing from the whole Christian Church. Such an enterprise, then, should from the very start be envisaged on an ecumenical basis and on an inter-racial basis. The world of activity into which such men will be going is one in which

denominationalism is totally irrelevant. Moreover, it is a world in which the distinctions of national culture and tradition are also irrelevant. Here might well be an opportunity for a new step forward in the whole task of the Christian mission in our time.[1]

After eleven years it has to be sadly confessed that not much has been done to respond to this call. It does not fit easily into the patterns of action which we have inherited. It requires a firm faith that the secular world of industry and technology is part of God's creation, ruled by him, and destined to minister to the fullness of the new creation in Christ. It requires equally a willingness to trust the Holy Spirit to lead us in new paths and to create new forms of fellowship for new adventures in obedience. A truly biblical understanding of the mission of the triune God must surely furnish these things.

A certain nostalgia for 'Christendom' is very human and understandable—whether in the countries of Western Europe which see the old ecclesiastical landmarks being more and more obliterated or else turned into museum pieces; whether in the old 'mission fields' where Christian schools and hospitals no longer have the leadership in national evolution; or whether in countries like Cuba where the old security of the Church is suddenly and dramatically removed. But we have to accept gladly the way God leads us, recognizing that a 'Christendom' situation can only be a temporary and passing phase in the mission of the Church and that the 'desacralizing' of great areas of human life is all part of the journey by which God leads the world to the ultimate issue of faith or unbelief in Jesus Christ. By participation in the life of the Spirit we are enabled to acknowledge his fatherly rule in this as in all things, to share that acceptance of the 'powers that be' which marked the life of the Son on earth, and to have the assurance which the Spirit gives in bearing witness to that victory within the life of a radically secularized society.

---

1. Norman Goodall (ed.), *Missions under the Cross* (Edinburgh House Press, 1953), pp. 31–2.

VII: The Pattern of Missionary Advance

Among the questions chosen for consideration in this essay the third is the one which touches most closely the nerve of missionary action. It is the question of the immobilization of the missionary movement itself, the question—in other words—of the failure of missions to produce, in the measure in which the Gospel should lead us to expect, spontaneously multiplying Christian communities among the peoples of Asia and Africa. It is, to put it in yet other words, the question: 'Why are the resources of the missionary movement today so largely exhausted in the support of dependent churches and why is so little energy available for fresh advance?'

Modern missions have proceeded for the most part along the currents of secular power. It was from the relatively wealthy and powerful nations that missions generally went, often to the territories which were at the same time coming directly under the political and economic influence of their mother countries. They had behind them material resources superior to those of the people to whom they went. They were able to use these resources to employ native agents, to buy lands and buildings, and to establish institutions of training and service modelled upon those of the sending countries. These institutions, being related to the economy of the sending country rather than to that of the receiving country, continued to depend heavily upon the resources of the missions that founded them. And, still more important, the newly established Christian communities generally depended from the beginning upon the support of the founding missions, both spiritually and materially.

So long as the political and economic power of the Western nations continued to grow relatively to the rest of the world, missionary advance could continue along these lines. But as the advance continued, the amount of support required also continued to increase and the proportion of resources available for fresh advance decreased. The whole movement tended to become immobilized by its own success. There are notable exceptions to this statement, but taking the whole modern missionary movement it is a justifiable generalization.

It was inevitable that this situation should cause comparisons to be drawn with the missionary methods of the first century. So far as the evidence of the New Testament enables us to understand them, the missionary methods of St Paul and his colleagues differed profoundly in many respects from what has just been described. Manifestly the apostles had behind them no predominant financial and political power such as was enjoyed by the missionaries of the nineteenth century. Nor did they have behind them the prestige of a so-called higher civilization. They were not going to 'under-developed areas'. They were in no position to offer 'technical assistance' to the citizens of Corinth, Ephesus and Rome. There is no evidence that they paid salaries to their converts in these cities to become 'agents' of the mission, nor do we read of any appeals to Antioch for additional funds to support the new churches and to make fresh evangelistic advances. The financial transactions of which we read are all the other way—gifts from the 'younger church' for the support of the apostle (e.g. Phil. 4:10ff), or for the relief of distress in the 'older churches' (2 Cor. 8–9 et al.). There is no sign of financial dependence of younger on older churches.

More important still is the fact that there is no sign of the kind of spiritual dependence with which we have become distressingly familiar in the story of modern missions. The younger churches of modern times have—in most cases—been dependent for ministerial leadership upon the founding missions for years and even decades after their first establishment. The churches established by St Paul, so far as we can tell from the available evidence, had their own ministry of elders or bishops

and deacons, as well as others, from the very beginning. They
were at no time dependent upon the older churches of Syria or
Judaea for the essentials of their life as Christian congregations.
They had, it is true, an abiding relationship with St Paul, which
he expresses by such phrases as, 'For though you have countless
guides in Christ, you do not have many fathers. For I became
your father in Christ Jesus though the gospel,' (1 Cor. 4:15). He
is their father in God, and he does not hesitate to remind them
of the fact when it becomes necessary. But there is no suggestion
that this paternal relationship is automatically bequeathed to the
authorities of the Church in Antioch. And the fact that St Paul
is so plain about it makes it all the more striking that he always
addresses even the most erring and sinful congregation as—in
the fullest sense—the Church of God. He does not address them
in the manner of a superintendent addressing subordinates. He
disclaims any thought of lording it over them: he is their
colleague, not their controller (2 Cor. 1:24). They have their own
free standing in the faith and he speaks to them as to adult sons,
members with him in the household of God.

It is these living congregations which become, in turn, the
centres of further missionary advance. They do not depend upon
the 'Antioch mission' for their support, and advance does not
depend upon increased resources from outside. They have in
themselves—or rather in the Holy Spirit who is with them—the
essential resources for witness and growth. There is no suggestion that they are 'secure' in a human sense, or that they can
enjoy any protection from the mother church. On the contrary
they are warned, at the moment when the apostle takes leave of
them after they have believed and been baptized, that 'through
many tribulations we must enter the kingdom of God'. But it is
precisely in the context of that warning that we read of the
apostles that when they had appointed elders for them in every
church, with prayer and fasting, they committed them to the
Lord in whom they believed, and passed on (Acts 14:23). If we
ask what is the secret of this extraordinary confidence, which
permits the apostles to ordain to the holy ministry men con-
verted only a few weeks before, to leave without any personal

supervision congregations newly won from paganism, surrounded by all the evil and corrupting powers of pagan society, without visible support and with, so far as we know, few men and women of influence and education among them, there can be only one answer: it is because they are convinced that these new Christians have received the Spirit. It is not too much to say that the whole 'method' of St Paul (if that be the right word for something which is far more than a method) rests upon this single point: that the Holy Spirit of God is himself the missionary; that his presence and blessing are given to those who receive the Gospel; that that presence and blessing are recognizable by those who have the Spirit; and that where the Spirit is, there is all the power and all the wisdom and all the grace that man needs or can expect for the life in Christ.

If, with many scholars, we accept the view that the Epistle to the Galatian's was addressed to those same congregations of whom we read in Acts 14, we have an exceptionally clear statement of the grounds of that confidence which enabled the apostles to take what—in the view of modern missionaries—would be regarded as the appalling risk of leaving new congregations without proper supervision. For here is a case in which the new congregations did in fact go astray very quickly. It might seem an important piece of evidence against the missionary method of St Paul. Certainly the very fact of the letter makes it clear that when the apostles committed the new congregations to the Lord and left them in charge of their own elders, they were not severing their links with them. Every paragraph of the letter bears witness to the intense spiritual solidarity of the apostle with these Galatian Christians, his deep love for them and his sense of responsibility for them. Yet the whole argument of the letter shows that he rests everything on his faith in the adequacy of the Spirit as the source of truth and holiness. The false apostles who have led the Galatians astray have every appearance of authority on their side. They can quote both Scripture and tradition with apparently overwhelming effect. St Paul takes them back to the Cross, interpreted through his own experience, and then asks them this question; 'Let me ask you only this: Did you receive the Spirit by the works of the law, or by hearing with faith?' Everything rests upon this assurance— that their being in Christ is a matter of having received the Spirit. When he goes on to meet his opponents on the ground of Scripture, it is to persuade them that the true sons of Abraham are those 'born according to the Spirit'. And finally he shows them that the real issue is not to be put in terms of law, but in terms of Spirit and flesh. There are two powers which may control us, the flesh and the Spirit. Those who are under the power of the Spirit have no law against them, for the Spirit himself produces in them that which the law commands but cannot give—love, joy, peace, patience, kindness, goodness, faithfulness, gentleness, self-control. These things are not produced by law; they are the fruit of the Spirit. And the Spirit is given by the hearing and believing of the Gospel of the Cross. Therefore Paul comes back in his autograph postscript to that with which he had begun: 'far be it from me to glory except in the cross of our Lord Jesus Christ, by which the world has been crucified to me, and I to the world.'

That is the apostle's answer to an erring congregation—not to devise means of bringing them under closer ecclesiastical control, but to remind them of the source of their life as Christians and of the place where they must go if they would be at that spring whence the life of God flows. In this epistle the reference is especially to the relation of the Spirit to the law. In other epistles—notably Romans, I Corinthians and Ephesians, much is said about the relation of the Spirit to the various ministries in the Church. Both of these have great importance for our understanding of the weakness of the modern missionary movement, and we shall look for a moment at each.

(*a*) No one who knows modern missions can doubt that one of the greatest problems confronting them is legalism, the tragic consequences of the attempt to achieve in new Christian communities conformity to an ethical standard by means other than the free assent of the conscience of those concerned. One hesitates to say much about this, for the subject is so full of both sorrow and perplexity. There are indeed some strands of humour in it too: who could read without laughing the stories of the struggle between missionaries in South India and their high caste converts about whether or not the traditional tuft of hair on the top of the head of a devout Hindu must be shaved off as a condition for baptism? But there is much more matter for tears. There is the tragic story, for instance, of the struggle against polygamy in Africa, where it has seemed that missions were trying to impose the rule of monogamy as a law before the conscience of African converts had awoken to the real issue, with the result that polygamy continues to flourish and the Church seems often to represent rather the company of those who have managed to evade it, rather than the place where victory and joy are given by the Spirit in the life of the family. Legalism is a besetting danger for Christians everywhere, but its dangers are multiplied when there is an authoritative organization, representing the superior power and prestige of the ruling race, standing alongside the Church to enforce by its many-sided authority the ethical standard accepted in the country from which the missionaries come. One cannot believe that St Paul would have recognized in this situation the kind of evangelical freedom in defence of which the passionate pleading of the Epistle of the Galatians was written. Have modern missions really acted as though they believed that the life in Christ, in all purity, grace and integrity, can only be a fruit of the presence of the Spirit and can never be the result of the impositions of a law? And does not the failure at this point account for much of the spiritual weakness, the attitude of dependence, that has characterized the younger Churches during most of the period of modern missions?

(*b*) No less central to our problem is the question of the Church's ministry. We have noted a startling contrast between the apostles, who apparently ordained the presbyters of the new congregations from among the new converts within a few weeks of their baptism, and modern missionaries who have generally thought that a period of some decades was needed before an ordained native ministry could be produced. Much can be, and had been, written about the reasons for this. There is no doubt that a great deal is due to the fact that the thinking of missionaries about the ministry was (naturally) shaped by the fact that the ministry in the Churches from which they came was a full-time salaried occupation for men of high academic attainments, who were accorded a place high in the scale of social influence. In such societies a ministry of shepherds, fishermen and tent-makers would have seemed impossible. But the attempts to transfer these sociological concepts of the ministry unaltered to the new congregations growing up, generally among village people, in the pagan societies of Asia and Africa, has produced absurd results, such as those not uncommon situations in which one man is nominally the 'pastor' of forty or fifty congregations. It has been difficult, in this situation, to take simply and seri-ously the apostolic belief that the Holy Spirit, who is able to call simple and unlettered men and women into the fellowship of the Gospel, is also able to raise up from among them the men and women needed for the manifold ministries of teaching, preach-ing, guiding, counselling and government. Consequently, unlike the churches described in the Acts of the Apostles, the younger Churches of the modern period have remained for decades dependent on their parent Churches for the supply of minis-terial leadership.

Surely there is no missionary who goes forth to preach the Gospel to others who does not know that it is only by the power and presence of the Holy Spirit that his words can accomplish anything. And surely there is no pastor who does not acknowl-edge that it is only by the work of the Holy Spirit in his congregation that holy lives can be produced. It may seem that in stressing the rôle of the Holy Spirit in the mission of the Church I am simply repeating what everyone knows. And yet I have become convinced that, even when this belief is present and vivid, there are factors in the structures and traditions of our work which can prevent the belief from becoming effective. I move at this point deliberately into the first person because I doubt whether what needs to be said can be said except in the form of personal testimony.

I have lived and worked as a missionary within the structure typical of modern missions, responsible for the conduct of institutions, for the supervision of Indian workers, for the employment and control of teachers and others in charge of congregations. I have seen this system come to a practical standstill: funds were not available to increase the number of salaried workers. New areas could not, therefore, be occupied. Teachers could not be offered to new villages. Enquirers who came to ask for a teacher to be sent to their village had regretfully to be turned away. Only if some fresh resources came from 'home' could the mission become a mission again. As it was, it was plain that any talk of 'winning India for Christ' was not serious. I was compelled to ask myself whether it is really true that the Church's obedience to the Great Commission is intended to be contingent upon the accident of a budgetary surplus.

The answer came through various experiences. Firstly, through seeing how ordinary lads from village congregations, removed from the situation in which everything was under the direction of the official agencies of Church and mission and living in the conditions of army life in North Africa or the Middle East, could themselves become active witnesses and evangelists among their comrades. Secondly, through learning to call on the services of all kinds of lay men and women as volunteer pastors and evangelists for the village congregations left without the guidance of a full-time worker. And thirdly, most decisively, through the experience of a small group-movement in a very backward area where the Gospel had only recently been preached for the first time. Out of the last experience certain clear convictions emerged which I believe have wide significance.

Firstly, it became clear that the decisive moment is the very first moment, when the first contact is made between the evangelist and the enquirer. In this area the Gospel was spreading through the witness of new converts. Groups would come from villages to which no agent of the Church had been sent, asking for instruction and baptism. The traditional response to such a request would have been to send (budget permitting) a salaried teacher to work among them and prepare them for baptism. Experience made it clear that there is another possible response.

It is to find out what the Holy Spirit has already done among them and build on that. Invariably it was found that, behind such a request, there was some experience which had prompted a desire to know more of Christ. It might be a dream, an answer to a prayer, a providential deliverance, the 'chance' reading of a tract or a scripture portion, contact with a Christian from another village. It might seem very insignificant. But questioning would bring out the fact that the Holy Spirit had, in this way, touched the life of a man or a group of men, to a new desire for God. That touch of the prevenient and sovereign Spirit must be accepted and acknowledged by the evangelist as his guide.

It follows, secondly, that the evangelist must acknowledge the person whom the Holy Spirit has thus touched as, for the present at least, the chosen minister of the Gospel to that community. It is a simple fact that the Spirit has chosen him; for it is through his experience that the group has come to ask for baptism. He may conceivably be an ignorant and illiterate man. This is important, but it does not prevent the Holy Spirit from using him, and continuing to use him. He has already a spiritual authority which the evangelist has no right to ignore. Specifically, he cannot be brushed aside, to be replaced by an 'agent' of the mission sent in to take charge of the community. It is he whom the Spirit has used to awaken in the group a desire for the Gospel, and it must be assumed until there is evidence to the contrary that the Spirit will continue to use him as their spiritual leader. Such help as is provided from outside will be by way of brotherly assistance; it will not replace the leadership which the Spirit has already provided. If the man concerned is illiterate, he can learn to read, and experience shows that a man who has been thus spiritually awakened will learn quickly.

Thirdly, once it is clear that the group has made the decision to turn from all trust in idols to the living God, baptism should not be delayed. Some instruction is plainly necessary, but it must not be such as to suggest that baptism is a kind of certificate of attainment. To maintain, as is sometimes done, that the enquirers should be placed under probation for a period before a decision is made to baptize seems perilously like suggesting that baptism is a certificate of good conduct rather than a laver of regeneration by the Spirit. Everything in the Gospel surely suggests that once the clear decision is made to turn to God, the Church should receive the new members of the Household with the same immediate welcome as Jesus gave to the sinners who came to him.

Fourthly, baptism must be followed by the fullest possible instruction. Experience shows that it is at this point that there is a real eagerness to learn. The attitude should be: 'Now you have been received into the Father's house; let us together learn what his household is, how we have been brought into it, how it is conducted, and what is the conduct which befits it and is pleasing to the Father.' But at every point it will be understood that the life of the new home is not the result of conformity to a law handed over by the evangelist; it is a gift of the Spirit who is himself the life of the new home, so that the new life is received by sharing in this life of the Spirit himself.

Fifthly, because this is so, learning and witnessing go together. During the months when the new congregation is learning the essentials of the faith, it is at the same time bearing witness among its neighbours. From the very beginning this is so, because what is being learned is not a lesson, but a life, the life of the Spirit himself whose very nature is to communicate. To put it another way, what is being learned is the love of God, and love is known in loving; therefore learning for oneself and communicating to others go together. The result of this, in the area of which I am speaking, was that the churches began to multiply themselves by a kind of spontaneous growth which was not dependent upon increasing outside resources. In an area almost entirely pagan, the number of Christian congregations rose from thirteen to fifty-five in twelve years. The secret of growth was the spontaneous witness of the new Christians themselves. And because the spiritual leadership was there, and not outside, the new congregations were proof against resolute attempts to destroy them by discrediting Christian missions. In the midst of a movement of this kind, one could speak seriously about winning India for Christ.

This small piece of personal experience is offered as evidence for the faith that the secret of the recovery of missionary advance lies in taking more seriously the New Testament understanding of the work of the Holy Spirit. Doubtless there are many features of the situation here described which are not typical of all the situations with which the Christian mission has to deal. But it is difficult to avoid the sharpness of the challenge which is presented to the conscience of any reflective Christian by the tremendous contrast between the missionary methods of the modern period and those of St Paul. It is difficult to doubt that modern methods have been, as is indeed natural, very largely shaped by the historical circumstances in which missionaries went from the Western world to Asia, Africa and other parts of the world. It is very clear that the era in which missions were an operation directed by the strong and wealthy Churches towards people relatively backward and ignorant is coming to an end, and that a pattern of missionary operations which depends upon the possessing of superior wealth, power and secular influence holds no hope for the future. It is therefore not surprising that in many places and in many ways the traditional 'work' of missions is being challenged by movements which seek to reproduce more faithfully the pattern suggested by the New Testament, and to stress more than missions have done in recent decades the primacy and sovereignty of the Holy Spirit in missions.

No one who has shared in such experiences as I have tried to describe can doubt the pertinence of this challenge. Faithfulness to the New Testament must bring us to give to the Spirit a much more central place not merely in the theory but also in the practice of missions. He is still sovereign and free—free to do the unexpected thing that astonishes us, just as Peter and the Elders at Jerusalem were astonished when his manifest presence was given to the uncircumcised Gentiles. He opens up ways that the missionary never expected, and when he does so, the missionary must follow. He chooses as his instruments people who would never have been selected by the missionary and when this happens his decision must be honoured. He makes out of very humble and insignificant people powerful witnesses in the face of hostile powers that daunt the ablest and most resolute Christian strategy. He uses apparently small and casual deeds and words to shake the powers of this world. He makes out of simple and uneducated people evangelists and pastors of whom the Good Shepherd himself will not be ashamed. He 'calls into existence the things that do not exist'. It is possible to be blind to his presence. It is possible to organize the work of missions as though the strategy were wholly in our hands. The things of the Spirit are discerned by the Spirit, and such discernment grows only with use. One can become progressively blind to them. But when one has grown accustomed to looking for his presence, one discovers that precisely at the moment when all the human factors seem to be stacked against us, he bears his witness and shakes the powers of this world to their foundations. He does not depend for his victories upon the superior resources of 'Christendom'. He asks everything we have, and uses what he will. If missions are indeed subject to the mission of the Spirit, then they need not fear, but should only rejoice if they are now called upon, after two centuries of working with the stream, to go against the stream, to go not from the rich and powerful of the earth to the poor and ignorant, but precisely the other way round. In such situations we shall learn afresh what that word means: 'It is not you who speak, but the Holy Spirit.'

Having said all this, one must now go on to say something more. There are movements in our time which lay such exclusive emphasis on the work of the Holy Spirit that they appear to be in danger of distorting their witness by failure to recognize that the mission is the mission of the triune God, Father, Son, and Spirit. There can, be a kind of monism of the Spirit which is not the faith of the New Testament. The recovery within the missionary movement of faith in, and experience of, the centrality of the Spirit in missions will be distorted if it is not within the context of the full trinitarian faith.

The Spirit is the Spirit of Christ. The decisive mark of his presence is the confession that Jesus Christ is Lord (1 Cor. 12:1–3; cf. 1 Jn. 4:1–3). His coming in power is the fruit of hearing and believing the Gospel of Jesus Christ crucified and risen. He takes the things of Christ and shows them to us. He leads men to Christ, in whom we are baptized into one body, the body of Christ. He is no will-o'-the-wisp, leading men on to all sorts of individual vagaries, but the one who binds men to Jesus Christ in the fellowship of his one body. It is true that he is free and sovereign; he goes ahead of the Church, as every missionary knows—but it is (if one may put it so) the Church that he goes ahead of. The word of St John is very decisive on this: 'By this you know the Spirit of God: every spirit which confesses that Jesus Christ has come in the flesh is of God.' The Spirit binds men to Jesus, to his historic life and to the fellowship of those who confess him as Lord. When this is forgotten, the name of the Spirit may be invoked to justify attitudes and practices which destroy the unity of the body. Mere vitality is not necessarily the mark of the presence of the Holy Spirit. Everything which grows vigorously is not thereby proved to be of God. The endless proliferation of new sects in the name of the freedom of the Spirit is not the same as what St Paul calls the building up of the body in love (Eph. 4:16).

The Spirit is the Spirit of God. He proceeds from the Father. It is by him that we are able to acknowledge God as Father. The characteristic utterance of the Spirit is 'Abba, Father'. By him we are able to believe that the fatherly rule of God governs all the events of human history, and to discern, in a measure, God's will for the secular life of mankind. By him we are able to live and act in expectant hope of the summing up of all things in Christ, because he is the foretaste, the earnest, 'the guarantee of our inheritance until we acquire possession of it' (Eph. 1:14). To have the Spirit does not mean to be withdrawn from the secular concerns of men, from the struggles of communities and nations for justice and freedom, from the labour of creative work in art and science. On the contrary, to be possessed by the Spirit will mean to share in the groaning and travailing of the whole creation which waits for its freedom, but it will mean that the groaning and travailing are filled with hope and with a sense of direction because the Spirit is the assurance of our adoption as children of God (Rom. 8:14–25). When the doctrine of the

Spirit is separated from the doctrine of the Father, one finds that younger people drift away from the fellowship because its life appears to be more and more irrelevant to the secular world in which they have to live and make their decisions. Thus movements which have begun by vigorous and liberating growth end in sterility.

It is necessary to say these things, because a recovered emphasis upon the centrality of the Spirit in the missionary task of the Church could be itself a distorted and misleading emphasis. The Spirit is the Spirit of the Father and of the Son. His work is to enable us to participate in Christ's Sonship, to be one with him in his obedience to the Father. And only he can enable us to participate in, and thereby be the occasions of, his witness.

VIII: A Trinitarian Understanding of Missions

The purpose of this essay has been to suggest that faithful dealing with the issues which press upon us in the missionary work of the Church requires an understanding of the work in terms of the whole Christian doctrine of God as Father, Son and Spirit. I have suggested that there is a danger in a kind of thinking which founds the whole missionary task solely upon the doctrine of the person and work of Christ and of the continuing work of the Church which is his body. I have given three illustrations of the way in which, as it seems to me, the doctrine of the triune nature of God helps us to understand and fulfil our missionary task in the face of issues which perplex us. Doubtless other examples will come to the mind of the reader. 'The doctrine of the Trinity,' says Leonard Hodgson, 'enables us to keep the right proportion in our faith.'[1] I have suggested in this essay that this truth applies also to our understanding of the missionary task.

It is rightly said that our missionary practice, when compared with that pictured in the Acts of the Apostles, suffers from an altogether inadequate trust in the reality and power of the Holy Spirit. It is rightly urged that the doctrine of the Spirit should have a much more central place in missionary thinking if missions are to recover their power of initiative. The example of the rapid growth of Pentecostal movements is adduced as evidence,

---

1. Leonard Hodgson, *The Doctrine of the Trinity* (Nisbet, 1943), p. 191.

and with justice. But, as has been argued, this recovery of a practical faith in the power of the Holy Spirit will lead us astray if it is not held firmly with an equally practical Trinitarian faith, a faith which discerns God's fatherly rule in the events of secular history, and which leads into full commitment to the life of that fellowship which is the Body of Christ in the midst of the world.

Similarly it is rightly urged that missions cannot deal with the realities of the life of men if they cannot help men to understand what God is doing in the revolutionary changes which are everywhere taking place in the life of the world. Thus, for example, the important Indian document, *Christian Participation in Nation-Building*, says; 'If the Church is to have a right response to the life of the nation, it is necessary for it to discern the presence and work of Christ in Indian nationalism, broadly defined as the inspiration of the nation's struggle for its selfhood.'[1] The full answer to this legitimate demand will only be found, as has been argued, as a trinitarian faith which, through the presence of the Spirit in the believer's heart enables him to trust the creative and providential power of the Father to direct all things towards the glorifying of the Son.

'The mission is not ours, but God's.' That phrase of the Missionary Assembly in Ghana must be taken with full seriousness. We are not engaged in an enterprise of our own choosing or devising. We are invited to participate in an activity of God which is the central meaning of creation itself. We are invited to become, through the presence of the Holy Spirit, participants in the Son's loving obedience to the Father. All things have been created that they may be summed up in Christ the Son. All history is directed towards that end. All creation has this as its goal. The Spirit of God, who is also the Spirit of the Son, is given as the foretaste of that consummation, as the witness to it, and as the guide of the Church on the road towards it. The

2. *Christian Participation in Nation-Building*, compiled by M. M. Thomas: Bangalore (National Christian Council of India and the Christian Institute for the Study of Religion and Society, 1960), pp. 294–5.

Church is not promised success; it is promised the peace of Christ in the midst of tribulation, and the witness of the Spirit given out of the Church's weakness and ignorance. For the future it has Christ's promise: '. . . it is your Father's good pleasure to give you the kingdom.' And for the present it has his assurance: 'Be of good cheer, I have overcome the world.'

Authors in the Biblical Classics Library:

Paul Barnett
    Bethlehem to Patmos (39)
    Is The New Testament History (33)
C.K. Barrett
    The Signs of an Apostle (19)
F.F. Bruce
    Men and Movements in the Primitive Church (13)
    The Message of the New Testament (1)
    The Pauline Circle (14)
David Burnett
    The Healing of the Nations (18)
Nigel Cameron
    Complete in Christ (29)
D.A. Carson
    From Triumphalism to Maturity (20)
    Jesus and His Friends (15)
    The Sermon on the Mount (2)
    When Jesus Confronts the World (16)
James Denny
    The Death of Christ (30)
    The Christian Doctrine of Reconciliation (35)
H.L. Ellison
    Men Spake from God (9)
    The Message of the Old Testament (3)
Mary J. Evans
    Women in the Bible (34)
P.T. Forsyth
    The Cruciality of the Cross (31)
    The Soul of Prayer (36)
John Goldingay
    God's Prophet, God's Servant (5)
Graeme Goldsworthy
    Gospel and Kingdom (4)
    Gospel and Wisdom (10)
    The Gospel in Revelation (6)
J.H. Greenlee
    Scribes, Scrolls and Scripture (17)